Private Rights & Public Lands

Edited By
Phillip N. Truluck

Acknowledgements

The Private Rights and Public Lands conference would not have been a success without the help of the four co-sponsoring organizations: the American Legislative Exchange Council, the Center for Political Economy & Natural Resources, the Pacific Institute for Public Policy Research, and the States' Rights Coordinating Council. To all of them, our thanks.

Special thanks are due to Jeremy Hobbs, who provided valuable editorial assistance during the preparation of the present volume.

Library of Congress Catalogue Card Number 82-84333

ISBN 0-89195-033-8

Table of Contents

Acknowledgements   ii

Foreword   v

THE PHILOSOPHICAL AND CONSTITUTIONAL CASE

Chapter 1
Introductory Address—Property Rights and Freedom   1
by Louis Pauwels

Chapter 2
The Law and the Land   9
by Bernard H. Siegan

THE BUREAUCRACY vs. THE LAND

Chapter 3
Reassessing Public Lands Policy   17
by Marion Clawson

Chapter 4
The Efficiency Case for the Assignment of Private
Property Rights to Federal Lands   29
by Gary D. Libecap

LUNCHEON ADDRESS

Chapter 5
The Federal Estate   39
by Senator Steven Symms

RECOMMENDATIONS FOR POLICY REFORM

Chapter 6
Energy Resources   43
by M. Bruce Johnson

Chapter 7

Privatizing Wilderness Lands: The Political Economy
of Harmony and Good Will   53
by John Baden

Chapter 8

The Case for Privatizing Government Owned Timberland   71
by Barney Dowdle

Chapter 9

On Privatizing the Public Domain   85
by Steve H. Hanke

Bibliography   89

Biographies   93

Foreword

"There is nothing which so generally engages the affections of mankind as the right of landed property."

—William Blackstone (1765)

The increasingly heated debate over environmental policy and public lands in particular has brought the rivalries among environmentalists, ranchers, recreationists, loggers, energy developers, miners, and others to a fevered pitch. Unfortunately, these political squabblings over control of the bureaucracies that dictate environmental policy have directed attention away from the most crucial dimension of governmental natural resource policy—how could natural resource despoilation have possibly developed despite the fact that nearly 750 million acres of U.S. lands have been in government hands for decades? Could it be possible that public ownership and management itself is a major factor, and hence *not* in the public interest?

Within recent years, the growing concern for environmental quality and conservation of natural resources has generated a fundamental reconsideration of the nature of government management of these resources. A growing number of environmental economists, legal scholars, and other experts have concluded that the public bureaucracies overseeing federal and state lands have been primarily responsible for the myriad economic and environmental problems which have developed. Much of this analysis is now available through the Pacific Institute's research book series, *Studies in Natural Resource Policy*. It demonstrates that the problems exist only to the extent that clearly defined, enforceable, and transferable private property rights to the land are absent.

At a recent conference in Washington, D.C., many of these experts were assembled to discuss in more detail these issues and the viability of pursuing privatization reforms for the public lands in the United States. The program attracted 200 Washington policy figures, and the issue of public land privatization has since been receiving increasing attention. Now, to facilitate a wider appraisal of public lands policy, we are very pleased to make the results of this important program available in this monograph, *Private Rights and Public Lands*.

Beginning with a discussion of the philosophical and legal setting of federal lands policy, the book focuses on the fundamental dilemma of public bureaucratic management of land in the United States. The volume then proceeds to contrast the implications of public and private ownership of land, emphasizing the related natural resource problems facing us today, and finally examines various strategies for privatization of energy, wilderness, forestlands, and rangeland resources.

We hope that *Private Rights and Public Lands* will be effective in creating a more responsible and enlightened debate over the problems of public land and environmental policy, and as a result, enable the privatization position to be better understood.

David J. Theroux
President
Pacific Institute for Public
  Policy Research

Phil N. Truluck
Executive Vice President
The Heritage Foundation

Property Rights and Freedom

by Louis Pauwels

First of all I would like to thank The Heritage Foundation not only for having brought me here, but for its support of the tradition of principles to safeguard the free world. I am very honored, moved, and surprised to find myself on Capitol Hill, among eminent economists and legislators. Perhaps it is with a sense of humor that I was invited to speak about the business matters of a country which is not mine in a language that is not yours. And, I am neither a legislator nor an economist: I am only a specialist in general ideas. It is a very widespread speciality, because it is the only one which can be acquired without any qualifications.

Today Europe, and particularly my country, is being seduced by socialism. In France, the nationalization of credit and of an important part of industry, the taxes which soon are going to reach 50 percent of the G.N.P., ever increasing government intervention in the system of production, schooling, information, and culture, the social and administrative sector submitting to the power of political unions, the dominance of leftist ideologies in the political and economic area—all those factors pull the country toward a collectivist society. We are rushing up the painful road toward socialism. I hope we will not go all the way. In fact, I even hope we will turn around. Do not be misled: socialism is none other than Marxism. It is only a confused Marxism that doesn't dare accept all the consequences of what it says and does.

I suppose that I was asked to speak to you because I belong to the large group of people in France who refuse to accept my country's move to socialism. We are very numerous, and as an intellectual, a writer, and a journalist, I am one of their spokesmen. On their behalf, I would like to say the following: America must succeed in its new beginning. The political-social philosophy and economic doctrine of President Reagan must succeed. You must show us that by reducing taxes and social costs, by limiting government intervention in the economy, and by lowering the regulatory power of the administration, you encourage the country's prosperity, increase national revenues, and offer new possibilities to all citizens, particularly the disadvantaged classes. You must show that in practice a policy contrary to socialism will obtain good results for all, and will advance justice and freedom.

Today we need to believe that Wilson was right at the beginning of the century when he said, "Freedom never came from the state. The history of freedom is the history of limitations imposed on government power." Today we need to believe that Walter Lippman was right when he wrote in 1937: "In a free society the government does not administer men's business, it administers justice among men who conduct their own affairs," and we need to believe that in his message of the 18th of February, 1981, your President was right when he said: "Those that make the economy work don't need the government to make rational and intelligent decisions to organize and conduct their own life." The values of freedom which are the basis of these simple and powerful statements are the same which initiated old European humanism. However, we Europeans are developing amnesia. We are forgetting and betraying these values without even realizing it. This is why we need to rediscover them in the light of what is happening currently in your country. It is the success of your experience that will help us recover our values, love them, serve them, and propagate them again. Similarly, we must follow with attention and sympathy the question that you are discussing today.

I read on this subject the supporting text of Senator Paul Laxalt. The Senator expresses surprise that in your country, which is based on free enterprise, one-third of all the land belongs to the state. It is a paradox and it is the indication of a drift. If I understood correctly, in addition to possible better use of the soil and subsoil, the sale of a reasonable part of these lands to private citizens would reduce the national debt and would benefit everyone. However, beyond these practical reasons, the conference today has as an objective to show the contradiction and incompatibility in a true democracy between private property and government property. You demand an end to this contradiction, and you ask that absolute priority be given to private property. This is very important, not only for you, but for the world. Once again, many Frenchmen and Europeans, grappling with the doctrines and methods of collectivism, are concerned. We wish you victory so you can serve as an example.

You asked me to speak about property rights and freedom. You know the famous sentence of a 19th century French revolutionary: "Property is theft." It is a sentence that has had a lot of effect, but in reality it means nothing; it is just a sophism. The corollary of property is free exchange, and free exchange cannot be called theft. However, this sophism founded utopian socialism. What does utopia really mean? It means nowhere. It is not surprising that a sentence that means nothing leads nowhere.

Another kind of socialism claims to be scientific. It calls for the collective appropriation of the means of production and, in the name of

2

class struggle, it claims that state property is the only form of property that leads to absolute justice. However, when we see the direction that our societies are taking and see that freedom is diminishing, we discover that government property is the legal form of robbing individuals. If the primary value of a democracy is the respect of individual freedoms, we must recognize that the foundation of individual freedoms rests in the right to private property. In fact, individual freedom and private property are inseparable. Actually, the right to property is freedom.

Luckily, French literature is rich enough to be contradictory. One of our greatest writers, Chateaubriand, wrote: "Make no mistake about this, without individual property no one is free. Property is our only personal defense, and property is nothing but liberty." When our common ancestors drew up the first declaration of the rights of man and of citizens, they included the right to property among the inalienable and sacred rights. It is amazing that international organizations accept the distinction between human rights and property rights. We note every day that it is in the countries where the right to property has been abolished that human rights constantly are crushed.

A Chinese proverb says: "Societies are like fish; they always begin to go rotten in the head." When ideas are putrefied, the entire social body will decompose. Let me give you an example of a rotten idea.

One of our socialist leaders, currently President of the National Assembly, said: "A socialist country is first of all a country of freedom, it being understood that freedom presupposes constant targeting at equality of social conditions." Through our misfortune in France, we will see that one cannot impose an equality of social conditions without reducing the exercise of individual freedoms. To confuse social justice and the standardization of social conditions is to commit a profound injustice toward those who are competent. And what kind of freedom is it, one based on decomposition and distortion of the ideas of injustice? Moreover, under the freedom and equality, there is a dark will. A people rushed into demanding ever more equality until they confuse equality with uniformity are almost ready to accept serfdom. By leading men to sacrifice their dignity for security, freedom for equality, and justice for hypothetical social justice, they are led to ask for more state power. And when men are led to expect everything from the state, they forget how to rely on themselves. With these simplistic ideologies, they prepare absolute statism. After all that, they have not made an egalitarian society. All there is, as Orwell said, is "a society of equals where some men are more equal than others." These latter constitute an arrogant oligarchy who claim to know what is good for citizens better than the citizens themselves. The citizens are enslaved by a political, bureaucratic, and state police class, which is allowed anything.

I am going to tell you a story: two little rabbits one morning met in

3

Kremlin Square. "Hurry up," said the first one, "quick pack, we are going away! They have just decided to arrest all five-legged rabbits." "But," said the second one, "all rabbits have only four legs." "Oh certainly," said the first, "but at any time they can decide that any leg is the fifth leg."

But let us come back to our world which is relatively free and where rabbits are still not worried for their fifth leg. There are, however, reasons for two-legged citizens to begin worrying. In a society of true freedom, the state guarantees and respects the principles of just individual conduct. In a society that claims to be socially just, the authorities have a growing power to tell citizens what they should do by placing an increasingly heavy tax burden on their income. In varying degrees, all of us are threatened by this danger. The danger in modern democracies is that we perceive less and less clearly the threat of the state to freedoms. As long as the poisoned belief—in which anything that the government does is good for justice and anything that individuals do is bad for justice—dominates political life, civil liberties will diminish and government will become closer to a totalitarian system.

I support the system of free enterprise and free market because, more than anything else, it favors progress by encouraging initiative. It is also the most favorable to the disadvantaged classes. This system is based on capitalism. The word capitalism was really imposed upon us by Marx. We do not dare use this word with sympathy in Europe because it has become synonymous with evil and it is despised by intellectuals and the media. Even so, I do not see why I should not recognize its advantages. In my country, in my generation, no self-respecting intellectual would ever defend capitalism. However, despite simplistic analyses that describe free enterprise as the exploitation of man by man, it is the only system that permits man's own free exploitation by himself to express his own creative will. Finally, capitalism has overcome all crises in which socialism doomed itself. This is why Japan and the United States are at the head of development. In my time, it has been to capitalist countries, and nowhere else, that men who were deprived of food, dignity, and freedom have gone to find refuge and help. After 65 years of applied Marxism, the countries of Eastern Europe would not survive today without agricultural, economic, and technological assistance from capitalist countries. Dynamism appears only among nations that respect and protect the economic, social, political, and cultural independence of their citizens.

I am not a self-respecting intellectual because I defend capitalism. In fact, this is what most of my colleagues say about me in France. However, the evil that is growing in Western democracies, which you are trying to eradicate in your country, is the belief that it is enough to create a law or establish a new public agency in order to resolve a problem or overcome a difficulty. In other words, we just increase the power of the

4

state. The true regime of a nation is not revealed by its constitution; it is revealed by the degree to which a state interferes in citizen activities. The greater the interference, the less democracy there is. There comes a time when people must ask the question: how can we live more freely with less state control? However, in your country, as in mine, a political cultural elite is convinced that the state must replace the citizens in most circumstances. They are convinced that the dynamism of freedom and the strength of statism can be joined successfully in one society. They say that the real solution is to find a compromise between free enterprise and Marxism. However, reality shows that the greater the public sector becomes in a country and the more a state grows, the more the overall growth rate of the country diminishes. Reality also shows that the state can confiscate the riches of those who produce and redistribute the remnants to those who do not produce. The government can spend more than it possesses, but it cannot produce wealth. Work, not the government, is the source of wealth, not for some, but for all. At all levels of the social ladder, faith in work, initiative, imagination, challenge, and the will of individuals is the most precious capital of a nation's economy. Individual freedom is the fundamental value. Any policy that threatens or compromises individual freedom should be fought.

Economic freedoms are the guarantee of civil and political freedoms, and there are no human rights without the right to economic freedom. Economic prosperity depends today on innovation, and innovation is always guaranteed with a free market. Prosperity does not come from administration, plans, or decrees. It comes from the free market. We know that planning and collectivization lead to poverty. In fact, it is the only revelation contained in applied Marxism. The real question for leaders in the democratic West is not how to be slightly socialist, but how to stop being socialist altogether. I also believe that the source of wealth, employment, and growth comes from the profit that is necessary for investment. Profit should not be considered a crime, but a good deed. When one leads public opinion to be suspicious and to condemn profit, it does not benefit anyone except the new dominant class. Of course, many people would like to persuade us that, except for government wealth, all wealth is wrong and unduly acquired. Most of these people have university posts that are subsidized by those who produce. With our work we pay people to tell us that we stole the money with which we are supporting them. Obviously riches can be the result of theft, and stolen wealth should be condemned and turned over to the police and justice. But wealth that is produced should be respected and honored. A society that confuses these producers of wealth with criminals finally is committing a crime against itself.

The point of view in which the government is good and honest, and the producers are dishonest and bad, is a distorted point of view. It destroys freedom and it insults all working people. Of course, it is becoming

5

a very generalized point of view now, but a point of view that becomes generalized does not have to become a reality. We must have the courage to reestablish truth even against the greater number of those who oppose us.

I remember that in the 60s, many of our avant-garde intellectuals in France had become Chinese without having left France. They saw China as a Marxist monastery with a billion men, and they found this admirable. For them, the Chinese model proved that revolution can change man completely. Mao Tse-Tung and his little red book had taken away all selfishness and all self-interest from the heart of the Chinese man. Thanks to the revolution, a merchant people had been transformed into a population of saints entirely dedicated to building the purest form of communism.

But I also remember having learned that Chinese leaders had decreed a campaign of exterminating all the rats in the big cities. Each Chinese person was asked to kill rats. To encourage this vast clean-up effort, each citizen was to receive some coin if he produced a certain number of rats' tails. Well, the number of rats' tails rapidly became greater than the foreseeable number of rats in each sector. The inhabitants of Peking and Canton had discovered a second job: they had begun to raise rats.

I, therefore, conclude that the great and definitive transformation of man will not occur tomorrow. I conclude that the sociology of peoples and human nature is stronger and more lasting than all political systems and all ideologies. The human truth was at the end of these rats' tails.

A battle is taking place in this world between two kinds of society and, in fact, two religions: the religion of collective man and the religion of the individual. Everything that I, as an old European, have just said shows that I believe in the religion of the individual. Since you also profess this religion, let us help each other. Perhaps not to cause it to triumph all over the world, but at least to protect it inside our own nations.

Inside our nations, a heresy is developing which advocates a false idea of equality and state despotism. To sway public opinion, the heretics label those who struggle for individual freedoms as reactionaries. Well, let them do it! Let them say that we are the horrible Right because we defend the principles of freedom and property. Words are not facts, and in fighting for the rights of individuals, we have no apologies to give to those who betray individual rights.

The right to authentic property is sacred. Representing the possessions acquired through our work, merit, and circumstances, authentic property is an expression of man's deepest identity—something needed as much as air and light. These material things are transformed by personality and thus raised to the dignity of a creation, in the sense of the desire of a man to leave on earth, through objects or enterprises, traces of his passage. It says that this man was not content to take advantage of life; he brought something to his and everyone else's life. He succeeded, in a small or great way, to build a world in his image in this world. He took a bit of God's power, and thus he made his possessions sacred. He was right, and to withdraw or impede such authentic property is a kind of murder—a spiritual murder.

In knowing this, you are trying to restitute to private property and free enterprise land now in the hands of the state. You do this, not in the interest of a few, but for the good of all, and to demonstrate an eternal truth. Your success, which will take on symbolic value, is very important. And that is why I have crossed the Atlantic to bring you my best wishes and to express the support of many Frenchmen who hope for your success.

The Law and the Land
by Bernard H. Siegan

Contemporary society far too often ignores the high priority accorded the use and the enjoyment of private property by the Framers of the Constitution. They sought to establish and preserve a society dedicated to private ownership and enterprise in order to advance both individual freedom and the common good. The role of government was to encourage and protect, not to deny or prevent, private ownership. Three portions of the Constitution address property rights: the original document without amendment, written by the Constitutional Convention of 1787 and ratified by the thirteen states in 1789; the first ten amendments, usually referred to as the Bill of Rights, passed by the nation's first Congress in 1789 and ratified in 1791; and the Fourteenth Amendment, framed by Congress in 1866 and ratified in 1868. As I shall explain subsequently, the Framers of all three documents had a common belief that government should have only limited power to control private property.

This concern for securing private ownership should not be surprising. A major purpose of constitutional government is to protect the individual from the power of government. Constitutional government is essentially a compromise between liberty and authority with a clear preference for liberty. In various contexts over the years, the Supreme Court has accordingly interpreted the Constitution as establishing liberty to be the rule and and restraint the exception. Although the contemporary Court has not applied it to property regulations, this formulation is highly appropriate to the role of ownership under our Constitutional system.

The protection of private property rights is rooted firmly in Anglo-American society. The earliest English charter of liberties, the *Magna Carta* in 1215 A.D., contains three references to securing ownership, including the famous chapter 39, which declares that no freeman shall be deprived of his freehold or his other fundamental rights except by judgment of his peers and by the law of the land. The due process clauses of our federal and state constitutions are essentially reaffirmations of this early guarantee of individual rights.

The requirement that the state pay just compensation for all property acquired from the public was part of English law by the first half of the sixteenth century.[1] Compensation seems to have been the regular practice in America during the colonial period. According to Professor William Stoebeck "[W]hile the British were scoundrels in a thousand ways, they never abused eminent domain."[2] The requirement of compensation signified a great triumph for individualism and personal autonomy. The state could not require certain individuals to bear an excessive burden when government acquired lands or buildings needed to serve the entire community. Also, the authorities were deprived of a means for penalizing those they did not like.

The United States Constitution was written at a time when ideas of natural law and social contract were accepted widely and were highly influential. Government was thought to be powerless to deprive people of the natural rights which are inherent in all people by virtue of their humanity. The right of property was considered a natural and unalienable right which government was obliged to preserve and protect.

John Locke, probably the most influential philosophical commentator during the revolutionary and constitutional periods, provided an intellectual basis for these ideas about natural law. Locke wrote that people sought sanctuary in political society because of uncertain conditions existing in the state of nature, where everyone who lacked the personal power to defend himself might be victimized by the unscrupulous and evil. People entered into the social compact and formed a society to stabilize those uncertain conditions. In doing so, they relinquished most of their personal "rights" to the government, with the understanding that government was limited to the protection of those relinquished rights. The government was responsible, therefore, for protecting life, personal liberties, and possessions. The government could not take any part of a man's property without his consent, or, in the case of taxes, that of his representative. Otherwise, the creation of government for the purpose of guarding property rights would have been senseless.

The view that preservation of property rights was a major objective of government was pervasive in the English-speaking countries in the eighteenth century. American and English political leaders considered the right of property a bulwark against authoritarianism. They valued this right as a guarantee of freedom, autonomy, and independence for the average citizen. They asserted that, if government could take away the property of an individual, it could exert enormous power over the people. Fearing loss of what he had earned or possessed, a man would be reluctant to speak, write, pray, or petition in a manner displeasing to

---

[1] William Stoebuck, A General Theory of Eminent Domain, 47 Wash. L. Rev. 553, 566 (1972).
[2] *Ibid*. at 594.

the authorities. A power over a man's subsistence, asserted Alexander Hamilton, amounts to a power over his will.[3] Thus, property was a foremost right because many other rights depended upon it. The right of property meant that people could work, produce, invest, and create, secure in the knowledge that, except for taxes, they could retain the rewards of their labor and ingenuity. If the government wanted to take their property, it would have to pay a fair price.

The valued position of the property right in America at the time of the Constitutional Convention is indicated by the fact that most states restricted voting to owners of real property. For many Framers, a freeholder was the ideal voter. Frequently, he was financially independent, with a stake in the preservation of established society. To safeguard and encourage freeholding, a society must also guarantee the freedoms associated with ownership, including the liberty to make contracts allowing property acquisition, use, and disposition.

Notes made at the Constitutional Convention show the Framers' strong dedication to the right of property. Believing that property rights have a tenuous position under representative government, the leading constitutional Framers often asserted, on the convention floor, the necessity of protecting them. James Madison attributed the convening of the Constitutional Convention less to the necessity of remedying the deficiencies of the Articles of Confederation than to providing some effective security for private economic rights. Gouveneur Morris, a Pennsylvania delegate and one of the most influential, spoke for himself and other delegates when he stated: "While life and liberty generally were said to be of greater value than property, an accurate view would prove that property was the main object of society."[4] Although not all 55 delegates to the Convention may have shared these views, the vast majority generally agreed that preservation of the property right was a major objective of government.

Today, we have lost sight of the intensity of feeling about the property right and we understand little of the dedication to private property that is so evident in reading the notes of the federal convention.

Concern over the protection of property and other commercial rights in the States is evident in the Constitution. Article I, section 10, prohibits the states from passing *ex post facto* laws or laws impairing the obligation of contracts, an essential protection for preserving property interests. Article I, section 9 contains another *ex post facto* clause applicable to the national government. The enumeration and separation of powers of the federal government likewise were intended to limit its powers over property and commerce.

---

[3] Alexander Hamilton, *The Federalist* no. 79.
[4] Max Farrand, *The Records of the Federal Convention of 1787*, 4 Vols. (New Haven, Conn. and London: Yale University Press, 1966), Vol. 1, p. 533.

The Framers expected the federal judiciary to exercise judicial review in matters involving civil liberties, primarily those securing property and other economic rights. They believed that the natural law was the highest legal authority, except as altered by the Constitution, and that it safeguarded the prerogatives of ownership. Thus, even without explicit constitutional authority, the Supreme Court over which John Marshall presided protected property rights by holding state infringements of vested property rights invalid because they were contrary to the principles of free government.[5]

During the initial years of federal constitutional history, and until the early 1830s, leading judges and advocates accepted the idea of natural rights and the social compact as the basis for constitutional decisions. In that period, and in the years prior to the Civil War, high or federal courts in many states held or expressed the belief that natural justice required fair compensation to be paid when private property was taken for public use. These judges did not need a statute or constitution protecting property rights.

The original Constitution, ratified in 1789, does not mention property rights. The explanation appears to be twofold: First, the Framers thought that the common law would secure this right as it had in England. At that time, Americans believed that the common law, as the embodiment of natural law, protected their fundamental liberties from violation by government.[6] Second, some jurists and scholars have maintained that the two clauses of the Constitution, forbidding federal and state governments from passing *ex post facto* laws, partially were intended to protect owners against retroactive laws divesting them of existing property rights. These authorities contend that the judicial decisions confining *ex post facto* clauses only to banning of retroactive criminal laws are incorrect, and are inconsistent with the desires of the Framers for a broad coverage that would include retroactive civil laws.[7]

According to Justice Joseph Story, who served on the Marshall Court (and is considered one of the nation's greatest jurists), "every statute, which takes away or impairs vested rights acquired under existing laws, or creates a new obligation, imposes a new duty, or attaches a new disability, in respect to transactions or considerations already passed, must be deemed retrospective..."[8] Consequently were the ban on *ex post facto* laws to include retroactive civil laws, government would be severely

---

[5] Fletcher v. Peck, 10 U.S. (6 Cranch) 87 (1810); Terrett v. Taylor, 13 U.S. (9 Cranch) 43 (1815).

[6] See Bernard Bailyn, *The Ideological Origins of the American Revolution* (Cambridge, Mass.: Belknap Press, 1967); Calder v. Bull, 3 U.S. (3 Dall.) 386 (1798).

[7] See Bernard H. Siegan, *Economic Liberties and the Constitution* (Univ. of Chicago Press, 1980) Chap. 3.

[8] Society for the Propagation of the Gospel v. Wheeler, 22 F. Cas. 756,767 (C.C.D.N.H., 1814) (No. 13,156).

restricted in its powers to curtail the use of, and return on, private property. The existing zoning system could not exist, since it contemplates continual changes in allowable property use as decreed by local officials. There could be no rent or condominium conversion controls. However, a 1798 decision of the U.S. Supreme Court determined that the *ex post facto* prohibitions apply only to criminal laws, a decision that has evoked criticism from some judges and judicial scholars.[9] Interestingly, two of the three Justices writing on the issue opined in part on the policy ground that an expanded *ex post facto* law would constitute too drastic a limitation on government. Thus, at this very early stage in the nation's history, our High Court may have overruled a major policy decided just over ten years earlier by the Constitution's Framers.

Specific protection was provided for property rights by the Bill of Rights, consisting of the first Ten Amendments to the Constitution. Historians generally agree that the original Constitution would never have been ratified had not its proponents promised subsequent support for the inclusion of a Bill of Rights. The "taking clause" in the Fifth Amendment, which states that private property shall not be taken for public use without just compensation, provides direct protection of property rights. Five other provisions in the Bill of Rights directly or indirectly secure the ownership of property: the Fifth Amendment states that no person shall be deprived of life, liberty, or property without due process of law; the Second Amendment prohibits the confiscation of arms; the Third Amendment restricts the quartering of troops; the Fourth forbids unreasonable searches and seizures; and the Eighth prohibits excessive bail and fines. Together, these provisions surrounded the ownership of property with a formidable protective shield.

The Fifth Amendment's taking clause codified the common law guarantee of property. William Blackstone, the most influential legal commentator at the time of the Constitutional Convention, defined the right of property as "absolute...[and] consists in the free use, enjoyment and disposal [by man] of all his acquisitions, without any control or diminution, save only by the laws of the land."[10] This right was "probably found in nature" but was subject to the state's powers of eminent domain (with full indemnification), of taxation (only by Act of Parliament), and of regulation (gentle and moderate.) Government otherwise could not obtain or limit interests in property. Blackstone emphasized in his discussion of eminent domain that the right of ownership was so strong that even public necessity must be subordinated to it.[11]

Thus, according to Blackstone, government had to indemnify an in-

---

[9] Calder v. Bull, 3 U.S. (3 Dall.) 386 (1798).

[10] William Blackstone, *Commentaries on the Law of England*, 4 Vols. (Oxford, 1765–1769), Vol. 1, p. 134.

[11] *Ibid*. Vol. 1, p. 135.

dividual for any property it acquired, and it could not impose any taxes on the people without their consent or that of their representatives in Parliament. Like the other "absolute rights" of life and liberty, property rights were subject only to "[r]estraints in themselves so gentle and moderate, as will appear upon further inquiry, that no man of sense or probity would wish to see them slackened."[12] Certain uses of property which caused serious harm to others, such as public nuisances and offensive trades and manufactures, were not protected by the law and were subject to fine.[13] Therefore, as Chancellor James Kent later wrote, government could interdict, without compensation, property uses creating nuisances or actual perils to the populace's health, safety, peace, and comfort.[14] Otherwise the use of property was largely secure from government regulation.

The first Ten Amendments of the Constitution apply only to the federal government. In 1868, the nation ratified the Fourteenth Amendment safeguarding the exercise of certain rights against deprivation or limitation by the states. Two clauses in the first section of that Amendment may be construed as securing property rights. These are the due process clause and the privileges and immunities clause. The due process clause is similar in language to the due process provision of the Fifth Amendment. It embodies, and makes relevant to the states, the common law requirement of just compensation, as had the taking clause of the Fifth Amendment in the case of the federal government. The other clause prohibits any state from making or enforcing any law abridging the privileges or immunities of United States citizens. Although the courts have not applied the clause for such purposes, many constitutional authorities have contended that the privileges and immunities of United States citizens include property and economic rights.

This was the view of the four dissenting justices in the famous Slaughter-House Cases. Decided in 1872, these cases were the first major interpretation of the Fourteenth Amendment. The four dissenters asserted that the privileges and immunities clause was intended, among other things, to safeguard the liberties to acquire and enjoy property and to pursue an occupation or business. The debates in the Congress that framed the Fourteenth Amendment support this interpretation. The reason the Court's majority of five in the Slaughter-House Cases did not subscribe to it appears to have more to do with national policy than with constitutional interpretation. These Justices were reluctant to extend federal government powers to actions by the states as the dissenters' position would have required.[15]

---

[12] *Ibid*. Vol. 1, p. 140.
[13] *Ibid*. Vol. 4, p. 167.
[14] James Kent, *Commentaries on American Law*, 4 Vols. (New York, 1827), Vol 2, p. 276.
[15] Slaughter-House Cases, 83 U.S. (16 Wall.) 36 (1872).

The Fourteenth Amendment is one of the most important provisions in the Constitution. Most deprivations of individual liberties occur at the local or state levels of government. Without the Fourteenth Amendment, neither the federal courts nor Congress could safeguard these liberties. The intent of its Framers is consequently of great importance in determining the constitutional status of property, which, it should be added, is largely regulated at the state and local levels.

Accordingly, we should understand that a strongly protective attitude for private property rights existed at the time the Fourteenth Amendment was framed and ratified. Illustrative of this position, Justice Samuel F. Miller in the unanimous 1871 decision in *Pumpelly v. Green Bay and Mississippi Coach Co.*, construed the taking clause of Wisconsin's Constitution as requiring compensation for the flooding of the plaintiff's land caused by the erection of a public dam. In this case, Wisconsin contended that the flooding did not constitute a taking by government and was an incidental damage to property not requiring compensation. The court disagreed in very strong terms. Justice Miller wrote:

> It would be a very curious and unsatisfactory result, if in construing a provision of constitutional law, always understood to have been adopted for protection and security to the rights of the individual as against the government and which has received the commendation of jurists, statesmen, and commentators as placing the just principles of the common law on that subject beyond the power of ordinary legislation to change or control them, it shall be held that if the government refrains from the absolute conversion of real property to the uses of the public it can destroy its value entirely, can inflict irreparable and permanent injury to any extent, can, in effect, subject it to total destruction without making any compensation, because in the narrowest sense of that word, it is *not taken* for the public use. Such a construction would pervert the constitutional provision into a restriction upon the rights of the citizen, as those rights stood at the common law, instead of the government, and make it an authority for invasion of private rights under the pretext of the public good, which had no warrant in the laws or practices of our ancestors.[16]

These, then, are the attitudes and opinions held during periods when critical portions of our Constitution were formulated. To be sure, they do not necessarily reveal how specific controversies over property interests should be resolved. But they are consistent with the position that the Constitution forbids limitations on private ownership except upon payment of compensation or when necessary to achieve vital and pressing governmental interests.

---

[16] 80 U.S. (13 Wall.) 557, 560 (1871).

15

3

Reassessing Public Lands Policy
by Marion Clawson

Publicly owned land is an integral part of the U.S. economy, life-style, and political structure.[1] Forty-two percent of the total land area of the United States is publicly owned. Public land is to be found in nearly every county, but the largest acreages are in the West. Land is publicly owned for many purposes: streets and highways; parks and recreation areas; reservoirs; military reservations; and many others. This paper focuses on the multiple purpose federal lands under the management of the Forest Service and the Bureau of Land Management. With some exceptions, these lands are multiple-use lands. Commercial use of these lands is often highly important.

The United States is regarded widely as the citadel of private property by ownership and private economic enterprise. A far more accurate description of our economy, and of the ownership and use of natural resources in particular, is that we have a mixed public-private situation. Many of our natural resources are publicly owned, but privately used; on the privately owned resources, the use is heavily influenced if not controlled by public action. Little private land in the United States is now free from governmental control or direct influence. This is most obvious in cities where elaborate planning and zoning activities restrict the permissible uses of private land, but environmental controls also extend to private property and affect private land use. Even agriculture, once thought to be the epitome of individual free enterprise, is affected greatly by federal crop loan, subsidy, and area restrictions or influences. The U.S. has a mixed public-private economy, and the dividing line between private use of publicly owned natural resources and publicly controlled or influenced use of private resources fluctuates.

The private use of public resources extends very much to the federal lands which are considered here: oil, gas, coal, and minerals are extracted from federal lands by private corporations and individuals, not by a

---

[1] William Stoebuck, A General Theory of Eminent Domain, 47 Wash. L. Rev. 553, 566 (1972).

federal agency or corporation; timber is harvested from federal land by private timber industry firms and individuals, not by a federal agency; cattle and sheep which graze on the federal lands are owned by private persons and companies, not by a government agency; and the extensive recreation use of federal lands is by private persons subject to public regulations. This public ownership-private use relationship is so pervasive in this country that it is often taken for granted.

Private use of federally owned land and associated natural resources has made federal ownership acceptable in an overall national sense. In the U.S., free private enterprise is not merely a slogan, but a reality. The ingenuity, inventiveness, and aggressiveness of millions of private individuals has created, and now operates, not only the vastly productive economic machinery of this country, but also the cultural and educational machine.

But this public ownership-private use arrangement is also basic to the policy issues and policy struggles that have characterized federal lands. If no private person used federal lands for any private purpose, there would be no policy issues about their management. Imagine a world in which no miner sought energy or minerals from federal lands, no one wanted to cut a single tree, no one wished to graze a single head of livestock, and no one wished to engage in outdoor recreation on the federal lands. Such a world is imaginary, of course, but differences in degree of use exist, causing differences in intensity of policy issues. In contrast, imagine a world in which all federal land use was by federal corporations which extracted minerals, harvested timber, and grazed livestock. While also unreal, such a world also would have its policy issues and problems.

Changing Role of Federal Lands

Although extensive federal ownership of land has characterized the United States throughout its history, the roles played by federal land in national policy and in policy conflicts have fluctuated greatly. Six major eras of federal land use policy can be identified. The eras overlap and the precise dates of beginning and ending may be debated.

1. *Acquisition*. The first era of federal land use policy involved the acquisition of land by the U.S. government. Some of the original states possessed claims to land outside their present borders, and as part of the political bargain among the original thirteen states, claims to western land (such as the Ohio Valley) were surrendered to the new national government, beginning in 1782. The Louisiana Purchase from France, the Florida Purchase from Spain, the war with Mexico and its cessation of the Southwest, the treaty with Great Britain and its relinquishment of claims to the Pacific Northwest, the Gadsden Purchase from Mexico,

and the purchase of Alaska from Russia brought extensive tracts of land to the federal government. Except for very small acreages already in private ownership, title was vested in the federal government: the U.S. government acquired political jurisdiction as well as property ownership in the private property sense.

The acquisition era is often assumed to have ended with the purchase of Alaska in 1867. Some recognition is given to land purchases under the Weeks Act of 1911 and the Land and Water Conservation Fund in recent years, since these (and other) Acts have permitted the federal government to acquire privately or state owned land for various federal purposes. The federal government has acquired extensive areas of "land" in the Outer Continental Shelf (OCS)—250 or more million acres—in the past twenty five years, by law and proclamation rather than treaty or purchase. People familiar with the more solid land of the West tend to ignore or downplay these OCS "lands." While few trees and little grass grow on them, the OCS areas produce oil and gas which is indistinguishable in end use from the oil and gas produced from dry land areas. They also produce vast sums of income for the federal treasury—income that states and counties would love to share, but so far have not obtained in significant measure.

2. *Disposal*. The 19th century was dominated by wholesale disposal of federal lands to individuals, corporations, and states under a wide variety of sale, homestead, grant, and other laws. About two-thirds of all privately owned land in the United States today began as private land in this disposal process. The disposal process extended until the passage of the Taylor Grazing Act in 1934. Perceiving a rush to homestead lands scheduled for inclusion in grazing districts, President Franklin Roosevelt withdrew virtually all remaining public domain from private entry.

Two aspects of this disposal process are evident on the federal lands today. First, before federal lands could be disposed of, they had to be surveyed, and the resulting cadastral survey left an indelible mark on the land ownership and use pattern in all the public land states. Second, the land disposal process was selective; persons or corporations took the best land available to them under law, within the limits of their knowledge, and under the economic and transportation conditions of the times. The result is the extensively intermingled land ownership pattern that characterizes much of the federal land today, and the attendant problems to both federal land manager and to private land user.

3. *Reservation*. The excesses of the disposal process caused large areas of federal land to be taken out of the disposal process and moved into permanent federal ownership. The first large withdrawal was Yellowstone National Park, followed by other national parks in later years. However, the first system of permanent federal land areas was the forest

reserves (now national forests), begun in 1891 and essentially increased to their present total area by 1910. The grazing districts formed after 1934 were another form of withdrawal which removed most of the public domain from easy disposal to private parties. The ambiguity of the phrase "pending final disposal" in the Taylor Grazing Act was resolved in the Federal Land Policy and Management Act of 1976, which declared national policy to be federal ownership of these lands unless their disposal provided a clear national advantage. That Act, and its predecessors, seemed at the time to resolve the federal ownership policy issue but what seemed "permanent" then seemed less so later.

The reservation process was as selective as the disposal process had been. Headed by Gifford Pinchot, the U.S. Forest Service sought and obtained the withdrawal of federal lands which had the best capability of meeting agency goals. If the withdrawals had taken place twenty or more years earlier, before large areas had been alienated from federal ownership by the disposal process, or had the withdrawals been postponed for twenty or more years until further large disposals had been made, the areas included in national forests would have been very different than they are today. When the Forest Service tries to develop comprehensive multiple-use plans for the areas in the national forests, the agency, its friends, and its critics should recognize that historical timing—or historical accident—has determined which areas should be planned and managed by the Forest Service.

4. *Custodial Management*. For a considerable period of time, there was relatively little demand for the products of the national forests. There was equally good or better privately owned timber more readily accessible, outdoor recreation was at a very low level, and in other ways the national forests were not in great demand. Their management was primarily custodial, involving fighting fires, keeping out trespassers, making a few timber sales, issuing grazing licenses and permits, and perhaps building a few primitive campgrounds. This process continued, but with increasing use of all kinds, until the end of World War II, when it gradually merged into the next era. Many of the agency attitudes and management mechanisms developed in this period continued into later periods when conditions were quite different.

5. *Intensive Management*. Intensive Management began in 1950, when federal lands as a whole produced greater gross cash revenues than their total expenditures, including investment expenditures. During this period, timber sales rose greatly in volume and even more in price, more oil and gas leases were issued, outdoor recreation increased greatly, and many other values of the federal lands also rose. The agencies faced an entirely different order of demand for the goods and services from federal lands, and their expenditures for management rose considerably. In the 1950s the national forests produced a net cash rev-

enue above operating expenses in all years but one, with a substantial net cash income for the decade. Between 1950 and 1960, the national forests produced more cash income than total management and investment expenditures combined. The Bureau of Land Management, with large receipts from mineral leasing, always has possessed a substantially larger cash inflow than outflow.

6. *Consultation and Confrontation.* The current era of federal land management also includes intensive management, but its other characteristics make it a new era of consultation and confrontation. The public's role in federal land management is the essential difference between the present era and the immediately preceding one. Today, public participation is prescribed by law, and many citizen groups and individuals skillfully assert their rights. New laws, new court attitudes, and new public attitudes have established lawsuits about federal land management as a common tool in the political arena. Conservationists and, to a lesser extent, industry have turned from the resource specialist to the lawyer for effective land use action. The management of federal lands today is greatly different than it was a generation ago: new forces have entered the struggles; new skills have been brought to bear; new actors have gained the stage; and federal employees face new problems. Whether one regards the consultation and confrontation era as highly desirable or as regrettably disruptive, the scene and the process have changed considerably.

The history of federal land policies has been marked by a rather curious mixture of static and dynamic concepts. Among the static concepts have been those of sustained yield, carrying capacity, wilderness preservation, and unchanged federal land ownership. Each has been based on the idea that some desired state or relationship could be brought into being and maintained indefinitely. The forest was to be managed to create a balanced age distribution of trees. Trees would grow, be harvested, and be replaced, cycle after cycle, irrespective of changing uses and demands for timber. Grazing land was to be stocked with animals and grazed at certain seasons to insure annual output at a constant level, cycle after cycle, regardless of changing economic and social times. Some areas were to be set aside, untouched, unmanaged, and undefiled by humans, to be preserved unchanged forever regardless of dynamic ecological processes; and other areas were to be designated for permanent federal ownership, regardless of economic, social, or political changes. While the static nature of these concepts often has been ignored, static resource management is often incongruous in a dynamically changing world.

As static concepts were being developed and applied, dynamic ideas also developed. While a concept or practice hallowed by long usage may not seem dynamic today, its development and early application was of-

21

ten highly innovative. In the late 18th century, a cadastral survey of land was a new idea, but today the cadastral surveys are taken for granted even by those who use them. While seen as commonplace today, the land records for the public domain were an enormously inventive step forward when first undertaken. Although deficient in many respects, the land records system was adequate for over 6 million persons obtaining patent to tracts of public land. Homesteads, where free land was given to the man or family who would settle on the land and improve it, were revolutionary in their day. Public landgrants for public improvements—railroads, wagon roads, canals, common schools, colleges, and others—were also innovative. Each of these ideas illustrates the innovation often found in federal land use policy.

The Future Role of Federal Lands

The role of federal lands has changed considerably in the past two hundred years, and it will continue to change in the future. In the last few decades, the tempo of change has increased dramatically. Acquisition and disposal have been nearly continuous throughout two hundred years of history, and reservation and custodial management have continued over the greater part of a century. But intensive management lasted less than a quarter of a century, and consultation and confrontation has thus far been an era of only a few years.

Additional factors foretell changes in the future role of U.S. federal lands. Use of federal lands has grown as more timber is sold, more oil and gas are developed, more coal is mined, and outdoor recreation increases. For some services and products, actual use has changed little, but economic and social demands have increased. For instance, while fewer livestock graze on federal lands today than did a generation ago, the demand for grazing land has increased. The amount of water flowing off federal lands and the numbers and variety of wildlife on federal lands may have changed little, but the values have increased. All of this is an inevitable result of more people, higher real incomes per capita, more leisure, greater desire for outdoor recreation, and a better educated and socially more sophisticated population. In the broadest sense, demand has increased for all land, water, and associated natural resources. Because there was little demand for it a generation or more ago, federally owned land has experienced the greatest relative demand increases. The trend toward greater demand for the federal lands will continue to grow, and it must be considered in any proposal concerning land use. People interested in federal lands today are generally better educated, more travelled, and better informed about natural resources than was the general public a generation ago. At one time, most professional land management expertise was found within federal agencies. Until World War II, the Forest Service was the prime employer for

22

trained foresters, and federal agencies were the chief employers of range management specialists. This is no longer true: many people who are privately employed or simply interested in natural resources are as knowledgeable as federal agencies' experts. Users of public land are no longer willing to accept uncritically the judgments or pronouncements of federal agency personnel. Increasingly, a federal resource manager must learn to use private professional competence in resource management. Management of public lands may become less the monopoly of the federal employee and more a task for the informed public—at least in planning, though not in actual management operations.

Because of the increased demand for the federal lands and because of the increasing economic importance of natural resources, the capital value of federal lands has risen dramatically in recent years. No comprehensive appraisal of those values has been made, but the estimated value of the lands and resources managed by the Forest Service and BLM today approximates $500 billion—half of the national debt. This value has increased 22 times, in constant dollars, since the mid-1920s. Without knowingly embarking on a program of saving and capital accumulation, the U.S. possesses a vast pool of capital invested in federal lands. Our situation, amusingly enough, resembles a desert sheikdom which has come into great wealth from outsiders' exploitation of its oil and gas. The federal government has never viewed public lands as a pool of invested capital; in their management, in appropriations for their use, and in our planning and accounting procedures, capital value of federal lands is ignored. However, this policy will not continue indefinitely. Many groups, fighting for a share of the federal dollar will increasingly challenge a system of land management that produces large cash deficits and provides little or no return on the large amount of capital involved. Federal land managers cannot continue to manage federal lands as if neither capital nor interest rates existed.

Was direct federal management of land use suitable when custodial management was dominant, and will it be satisfactory for increasingly intensive and competitive management of these same lands? As noted earlier, many of the present practices, attitudes, and processes developed when management was custodial, and questions may well be raised as to their suitability today when management has become intensive and consultive-confrontational. The future surely will pose more difficult problems. Many groups and individuals are expressing concern about current management decisions and practices on federal land and the suitability of the processes by which such decisions are reached.

Directions and Forms of Future Change

While many agree that the present management of the federal lands is not fully satisfactory, there is no consensus regarding solutions to federal land problems. There are several possible alternatives:

1. *Improved Federal Land Management*. The federal government could retain ownership of federal lands and institute management improvements for federal lands. The Renewable Resources Planning Act of 1974, the National Forest Management Act of 1976, and the Federal Land Policy and Management Act of 1976 moved in this direction. In each case, laws were established providing relatively explicit directions to the federal agencies regarding management of the lands under Forest Service and BLM direction. Of course, the legislation represented compromises among numerous interest groups, including the involved agencies. There was substantial ambiguity in the legislation because more explicit directives would have been unacceptable to certain interest groups. The full meaning of the Acts slowly will be determined by the courts: the full meaning of the 1897 Act was determined only in 1974. If the Acts had been passed earlier, they would have been major pieces of statesmanship: the 1976 NFMA in 1960 instead of the Multiple Use Act and the 1976 FLPMA in 1934 instead of the Taylor Grazing Act. Congress frequently acts on a felt and evident need, and the effectiveness of its action often is lost. This is one of the strongest arguments against continued federal land ownership.

In the land management Acts, Congress demanded new, more efficient management of federal lands; the Acts called for intensive planning of federal lands, specification of forms of public participation, and establishment of economic criteria for the management of the resources. While the Acts called for improved management, no one, including the agencies personnel, is satisfied entirely with the planning and management which has developed. Many critics believe that, unless the planning and management of federal lands is made simpler, faster, more efficient, and more easily understood, the pressures for new land and resource management will grow until a drastically different policy is adopted.

2. *Land Transfer to the States*. Some or all of the federal lands could be transferred to the states, either free of charge, or with some kind of down payment or continuing revenue sharing. This is one suggestion from the Sagebrush Rebellion. Advocates believe that in contrast to the federal government, state governments would manage lands more efficiently, more effectively, and with more responsiveness to local needs and interests. Responsiveness to local needs most upsets opponents of the Sagebrush Rebellion because they fear the loss of hard won federal land "conservation" victories.

There is precedent for turning large areas of land from federal to state control: the common school grants; the quantity grants for colleges and other purposes; and the swamp and overflowed land grants turned large acreages from the federal government to the states. The states generally have a proved record of failure in land management. A review of the history of state land grant administration shows that virtually

24

every state has had a major political scandal concerning state land administration, and most states have squandered their land inheritance by sale or other disposition without adequate or reasonable compensation. Disposition of federal land to the states would adopt the worst of both worlds: a public agency, but state instead of federal, and public ownership instead of private.

3. *Land Transfer to Private Individuals and Corporations*. A substantial amount of federal land could be transfered to private individuals or corporations. The precise terms of such transfer, including the prices to be paid, the kinds of land available, the continuing restrictions on land use, if any, and many other aspects of such transfer would pose many policy questions. While most observers immediately conjure up the disposal of the most productive lands to profit-seeking persons or corporations at bargain prices, the possibility exists for transfer of other lands to conservation groups or other private but nonprofit groups. If The Nature Conservancy can be the recipient of a gift of private land, why not let it be the recipient of a gift of federal land? While some conservation groups have never sought ownership of land, others have, and all might be potential purchasers of federal land. Arguments for private ownership of land rests on the long proved capacity of individuals or groups to seek their own ends of income or satisfaction with more efficiency than public agencies. One version of the Sagebrush Rebellion calls for the transfer of federal lands to private ownership. Some also believe that the sale of federal lands could reduce the national debt. While some selective disposal of urban and rural federal property would be beneficial, sums that might be realized would not reduce greatly the federal debt.

4. *Mixed Public-Private Corporations*. Mixed public-private corporations could be established to take over the management of selected areas of federal land. Robert Nelson has proposed corporations for the prime timber-producing federal land, where initially 25 percent of the stock would be held by local governments (which now receive 25 percent of the revenues from some federal land) and the remaining 75 percent initially would be held by the federal government. The federal government's stock gradually would be sold to private persons or corporations until the corporation would be largely if not wholly private-local government.[2] Dennis Teeguarden has suggested mixed public-private corporations for the management of the national forests; each corporation would be self-financing and would make a significant interest return to the Federal Treasury.[3] Presumably the corporations would be responsive to local interest and concerns. The precise terms of the charters for

[2]*Ibid*. at 594.
[3]Alexander Hamilton, *The Federalist*, No. 79.

such corporations, the limitations, if any, on stock transfers, the kinds of land and the terms of the land transfer, and many other features of such corporations would pose policy issues which could be settled only after political debate. Although the general idea of mixed public-private corporations is not new, it has not been applied to federal lands.

Establishment of mixed public-private corporations for some types of federal land would not preclude other arrangements, including continuation of present arrangements, for other federal land. Indeed, Nelson specifically proposes other arrangements for lands not included in such corporations.

5. *Long-Term Leasing*. Long-term leasing of some federal lands might be regularized and extended substantially. Federal lands often are transferred to private parties on a limited basis: a family which picnics in a Forest Service or BLM recreation area enjoys exclusive use of a small site for an hour or two; overnight campers have a site for a little longer; ranchers have ten-year grazing permits; timber firms buy a major part of the value of a site with a very few years in which to harvest the timber; oil companies lease federal lands for defined periods of time; and there are other time related or space limited transfers of federal to private management. Time constrained transfers of control over specific tracts of federal land could be greatly extended, formalized, regularized, and made more appropriate for various types of natural resources. Terms of the leases should make them attractive and feasible for wilderness, recreation, wildlife, and watershed management groups, as well as for commercial use.

All federal land should not be leased out to various groups such as industries, ranchers, or conservation organizations. Probably less than one-fourth of the present federal estate would interest any group, and the remaining unleased areas would continue to be managed by the federal agencies under present laws and present (or revised) procedures. No one could be forced to lease, although the terms of leases could be made attractive and the risks of not leasing could apply some pressures on particular groups. The terms of the leases would have to be drawn carefully to avoid controversy and litigation, to promote efficiency, and to insure equity. Leasing of all kinds of private property for all kinds of uses is an established and widely practiced form of land tenure, and the lessons learned from private leasing could be applied to federal land leasing. Clearly, there are many policy issues that would have to be debated and settled before an augmented federal land leasing system could be put into operation.

For each of these alternatives, except possibly the first one, the operations would be selective as to types and locations of land and other resources. States might be reluctant to take over some federal lands, and much land probably would be unattractive for private ownership, mixed public-private corporation ownership, or long-term leasing. The selective character of past land disposals and past reservations of federal land probably could continue and could be governed by law or regulations. For instance, large blocks of highly productive forest land could be leased for long periods, but timber harvest could be precluded from less productive forest lands if leased for other purposes. Prospective buyers or lessees would classify the federal lands as suitable or unsuitable for the uses they sought.

Within the proposal for extended and regularized long-term leasing of federal lands to all kinds of organizations, a concept called pullback could be included. One person, group, corporation, or unit of local government might apply for a lease of a particular area of federal land under conditions of land productivity, size of minimum area, and annual rentals. Other persons, groups, corporations, or units of local government would have the privilege of pulling back, or taking over for themselves, up to one-third of the specified area. Whoever exercised the pullback privilege would have to meet the terms applicable to the original application, but the consent of the original applicant or of a federal agency would not be required. The pullback privilege would be absolute, not subject to discretionary approval or rejection by anyone. If there were more pullback applicants than could be accommodated under the one-third limitation, competitive bidding could be established.

The pullback concept would promote meaningful competition and bargaining among possible rival uses and users of the federal land. In many ways, it would be similar to the workings of the private competitive market. If a timber firm would apply for an area, a wilderness, recreation, or wildlife group could pullback to one-third of the area. The second group would have to pay the same rental or other cost as the timber firm, but the consent of the original firm would not be required. Likewise, a conservation group might apply for a wilderness area, from which a timber firm could pullback as much as one-third of the area. The necessity of paying the same amount as the original applicant would exercise a sobering influence on potential users of the pullback, while the vulnerability to pullback by others would impose a discipline on the original applicant.

These proposals for federal land use policies involve different terms for highly productive forest land than for less productive forests: the less productive forests would be available for long terms without initial cash payment and for nominal annual rentals, but timber harvest would be forbidden and lessees would have to pay all management costs. Additional terms could make the particular leases stiff but reasonably attractive on some kinds of land and wholly uneconomic on other kinds of land.

Major changes in federal land management seem likely in the future. The direction and the specifics of the change are less clear. Federal lands are an increasingly valuable resource and their management must be efficient, responsible, and economically sound. Although many alternatives exist, the problems of present federal land management seem overwhelming to many observers. Today, we are no less imaginative or less resourceful than were the men and women who pressed for the establishment of the national forests, national parks, and grazing districts. We too can innovate: let us try.

4

The Efficiency Case for the Assignment of Private Property Rights to Federal Lands

by Gary D. Libecap

Nearly one-third of the land in the United States, 740,000,000 acres, is federally owned. While scattered throughout the country, concentrations of federal land are centered in western states: 89 percent of Alaska; 86 percent of Nevada; 64 percent of Utah and Idaho; 52 percent of Oregon; and 48 percent of Wyoming. In six other states, federal lands are over 29 percent of the area. Of the 740,000,000 acres held by the federal government, 25 percent is administered by the Department of Agriculture, 70 percent by the Department of Interior, and 4 percent by the Defense Department.[1] These statistics underscore the enormity of federal holdings and the importance of decisions regarding tenure arrangements to them.

This paper begins with an analysis of past federal policies to determine why so much land was reserved by the government. Of concern is whether retention was based on public good arguments or other efficiency considerations. If so, then those considerations must be weighed in any proposed future transfer of land from government control. Section II of the paper outlines the theoretical impact on the level of production and wealth in the economy of both bureaucratic administration and private decision making under secure property rights. The section also provides a summary of available empirical evidence on the impact of bureaucratic land management.

I. *Federal Land Policies*

From 1785 through 1891 federal land policy had two goals: to facilitate agricultural settlement and to raise revenue. The rankings switched from time to time in response to the size of the federal debt and to political pressure from land claimants. Nevertheless, both aims led to the

---

[1] These figures are drawn from The Department of the Interior, *Public Lands Statistics* (Washington, D.C.: Government Printing Office, 1979).

rapid transfer of federal land to private individuals. The most common early transfer mechanisms were: auctions; direct cash sales at fixed prices (generally $1.25 per acre); military script issues to soldiers from the Revolutionary War, the War of 1812, the Mexican-American War, and various Indian conflicts; and land donations to states and firms for improvements including canals, railroads, and schools.[2] Early exchanges, other than script and donation, were in depreciated federal securities that retired the debt and lowered the real price of federal land. After 1862, homestead claims became the principal means for assigning title. The General Land Office in the Interior Department was created to process the transfer of federal land to private claimants, and land offices were opened throughout the frontier. These offices were staffed by registers and receivers whose salaries depended in part on the volume of local land sales; they received $1/2$ of 1 percent of the value of district land sales. Under this arrangement, the land east of the 100th meridian, running from North Dakota to Texas, was transferred to private owners. There were continuing distributional conflicts among claimants for federal land, and those conflicts helped to shape the laws passed by Congress. For example, the Preemption Act was enacted in 1830 to give actual settlers preferred access to land prior to auction sales, allegedly to protect them from speculators. Despite these conflicts, the fundamental aim of assigning private property rights was never seriously questioned. As late as 1880, the Public Lands Commission *Report* called for the more rapid granting of title as a means of safeguarding land from excessive and wasteful use. The commission and those it interviewed clearly understood common property problems.

The break in the trend towards privatization occurred late in the 1880s as the agricultural land laws became increasingly inappropriate for western timber and range land. Title could no longer be transferred as smoothly as before, delaying the assignment of property rights. For example, Congress restricted the assignment of private property rights to timber land to 160 acres per claim. In general, ownership of 160-acre plots could be obtained only by *bona fide* settlers for domestic use under the Preemption, Homestead, and Timber and Stone Laws, and there was no way for lumber companies directly to procure large sections of land from the government. To acquire the land necessary for large-scale logging operations, lumber firms hired entrymen posing as farmers to appear to comply with the settlement provision of the laws. Upon receipt from the General Land Office, the title was passed from entrymen to the lumber companies. However, the use of fraud was costly, since real resources were used to evade the law. For the Pacific North-

---

[2] For detailed discussion of the land laws see Paul W. Gates, *History of Public Land Law Development* (Washington, D.C.: Public Land Law Review Commission, 1968).

west alone, the cost of evading restrictive land laws from 1881 to 1907 was approximately $17,000,000, a figure greater than the total receipts received by the government for land sales in the region.[3] Moreover, when added to the government price of the land, these costs delayed the assignment of clear property rights for as much as six years. During that time the land remained open access and vulnerable to rapid cutting and other forms of excessive use. While these figures concern the Pacific Northwest, they are representative of the general problem facing potential timber claimants throughout the West.

The obstacles for obtaining property rights to rangeland after 1880 were similar. Because of arid conditions and low carrying capacity, viable ranches required more than the 160 acres authorized under the Homestead Act and similar land laws. With 25 acres commonly necessary to sustain one cow or five sheep for a year, and the existence of economies of scale, over 1,000 acres were required per ranch. Yet, individual ranchers had limited legal means for obtaining title to such acreage. Accordingly, most of the land was used without formal arrangements to control entry or to assign costs and returns.[4] The problem was recognized early. The 1880 Public Lands Commission urged adoption of 2,560-acre homesteads and cash sale of rangeland at a minimum of $12\frac{1}{2}$ cents per acre. No action was taken except for the 1909 and 1916 revisions of the Homestead Act, which minimally relaxed the acreage constraints to 320 and 640 acres respectively. In 1934, over 165,000,000 acres, 22 percent of the land area of the eleven far western states, remained unreserved and unappropriated under the strict land laws. In that year, the Taylor Grazing Act was passed, placing the range under the jurisdiction of the Interior Department and initiating formal grazing permits to limit entry and stocking.

Timber and rangeland are the primary components of existing federal holdings, and federal land policies after 1880 retarded the assignment of property rights, leaving vast tracts of land under federal control. Except for minor adjustments in the Homestead Act, there were no revisions in the 160-acre settlement policy, in recognition of changing western land conditions. In 1891, the General Revision Act repealed the Preemption Law and created federal forest reserves that could not be claimed. The Forest Management Act of 1897 provided the basis for permanent bureaucratic control of the land, formally reversing the

---

[3] Analysis of these restrictions is provided by Gary D. Libecap and Ronald N. Johnson, "Property Rights, Nineteenth Century Federal Timber Policy and the Conservation Movement," *Journal of Economic History*, 1979, 39, 129–142.

[4] For discussion see Gary D. Libecap, "Bureaucratic Opposition to the Assignment of Property Rights: Overgrazing on the Western Range," *Journal of Economic History*, 1981, 41, 151–158, and Gary D. Libecap, *Locking up the Range: Federal Land Controls and Grazing* (Cambridge: Ballinger, 1981, Pacific Institute Policy Studies).

century-old policy of transfer to private claimants. In 1907, President Roosevelt temporarily suspended processing of private land claims, and, by 1909, he had set aside nearly 195,000,000 acres of timber land in the National Forests.

This dramatic shift in federal policy came at the urging of conservationists such as Bernhard Fernow and Gifford Pinchot, advocates of scientific, bureaucratic management of natural resources. The assignment of private property rights provided an obstacle to centralized bureaucratic control. In advocating the creation of the forest reserves, conservationists charged that private lumbermen in the lake states of Michigan, Wisconsin, and Minnesota harvested too rapidly under the mistaken belief that timber supplies were inexhaustible.[5] Fernow and Eagleston, both Chiefs of the Division of Forestry in the Department of Agriculture, charged that the forest reserves were needed to protect the "magnificent forests of the West" from the onslaught of private harvesting. Fernow claimed that:

> ...the forest resource is one which, under the active competition of private enterprise, is apt to deteriorate...that the maintenance of continued supplies as well as of favorable conditions is possible only under the supervision of permanent institutions with whom present profit is not the only motive. It calls preeminently on the state to counteract the destructive tendencies of private exploration.[6]

Despite the claims of conservationists, there is no evidence that the harvest practices of firms were inconsistent with wealth maximization. Stumpage prices from 1890 through 1934 indicate no systematic overcutting or ignorance of market demand and supply conditions. Contrary to the allegations of conservationists, the historical record shows that large timber companies in the lake states and in the Pacific Northwest withheld production in anticipation of higher future prices. In a statement inconsistent with general conservationist assertions, Pinchot condemned major timber companies for not producing. Embedded in the philosophy of the conservationists was the concept of sustained yield where the amount cut should equal the amount grown. At the turn of the century harvest rates greatly exceeded growth. But contrary to the arguments of conservationists, wealth maximization does not imply that growth should equal cut.[7] The forests encountered by the early

---

[5] Analysis of Great Lakes area timber harvest practices is provided by Ronald N. Johnson and Gary D. Libecap in "Efficient Markets and Great Lakes Timber: A Conservation Issue Reexamined," *Explorations in Economic History*, 1980, 17, 372-385.

[6] Quoted in Johnson and Libecap, "Efficient Markets."

[7] It is important to note that Pinchot planned for scientific bureaucratic management of both federal and private timber land. See Gifford Pinchot, *Breaking New Ground* (New York: Harcourt, Brace, Jovanovich, 1947, reissue Seattle: University of Washington Press, 1972).

loggers were mainly old growth timber where growth was essentially zero. Harvest of those trees was a first step toward growing more timber, and slower harvest rates would have reduced the value of timber land.

Though lacking theoretical and empirical support for their position, the conservationists succeeded in reserving nearly 200,000,000 acres of forest land and creating a permanent agency, the Forest Service, for bureaucratic management. Both the agency and its advocates were successful in promoting central bureaucratic control. Fernow, Eagleston, Pinchot, and others assumed high-level administrative positions in the Forest Service, and the agency grew rapidly. Transferred to the Department of Agriculture in 1905, the Forest Service by 1909 passed by the much older General Land Office. It rose from a budget of $398,000 (in current dollars) and a staff of 821 in 1905 to a budget of $15,000,000 and a staff of over 2,500 in 1933. In a study of the budget growth from 1950-1980 of federal agencies responsible for managing natural resources, the Forest Service ranked at or near the top.[8] Between 1955 and 1980 its annual rates of budget growth, adjusted for inflation, were 6.2 percent.

The important bureaucratic goals of reserving land from private claimants also is evident in rangeland allocations. Despite evidence in the 1880s that the land laws were too rigid for arid western conditions, the General Land Office in the Interior Department opposed any modification in the Homestead Act to allow significantly larger tracts to be claimed. Moreover, the Interior Department vigorously prosecuted ranchers attempting to circumvent the land laws, and removed fences placed on the range to control grazing. Fences were removed from over 28,000,000 acres of land, leaving them open for overgrazing.[9] The General Land Office and the Interior Department endorsed the allotment of federal land for small farms through homesteads. Efforts by Interior to expand homesteading in the 20th century via legislative changes were successful. Over 1,500,000 claims for 314,000,000 acres were filed from 1901-1933, exceeding the 1,400,000 claims for 188,000,000 acres from 1863-1900. There was an important motivation behind the advocacy of homesteading by Interior. The General Land Office was the agency established to process homestead claims; the granting of larger tracts to ranchers would have reduced the total number of claims to be processed and led to the more rapid disposal of federal land, shortening the life of the agency. The increased homesteading after 1900 coincided

---

[8] Forest Service budget growth and bureaucratic goals are analyzed by Ronald N. Johnson "Budget Maximization and Agenda Control: The Case of the U.S. Forest Service," Working Paper, Department of Economics and Agricultural Economics, Montana State University, Bozeman, 1982.

[9] See Libecap, *Locking Up the Range*, Chapter 4.

with greater budget appropriations and staff for the General Land Office, and larger fee incomes for employees of land offices. Average appropriations, in 1967 dollars, from 1875 to 1900 were $6,300,000 and from 1901 to 1925, $8,000,000. Staffing rose from 1,026 in 1897 to 1,502 in 1917, and fee income increased from an annual average of $4,100,000 for 1881–1900 to $5,100,000 for 1901–1920. After 1920, however, land disposal became less rewarding for the Interior Department. Claiming dropped sharply as the failure of dryland homesteads signaled the final limits of agricultural settlements on the remaining federal land. Appropriations, fee and commission income, and staff for the General Land Office correspondingly fell. By 1932, the agency's budget had fallen to $5,000,000 in 1967 dollars, fees to $700,000, and staff to 641.[10] By contrast, allocations for the Forest Service were expanding, revealing that management of land had become a source of greater budget appropriations than disposal. The differing fortunes of the Forest Service and General Land Office could not have been missed by officials in the Interior Department. Rather than lobbying for recognition of rancher claims as homesteading diminished, Interior officials entered into competition with the Department of Agriculture for control of the western range. After 1920 the Interior Department shifted from its historical emphasis on land distribution to advocacy of permanent bureaucratic management. The turnabout in Interior's position is reflected in Secretary Wilbur's call for planning and rejection of market processes in 1930: "The adjustment of a people to its environment can take place through a thoughtless struggle in the survival of the fittest, or it can be a planned, quiet, and orderly process of human organization."[11] From 1920 to 1934 Congress annually considered competing proposals from both departments for control of the 165,000,000 acres of unappropriated rangeland. Even after the 1934 enactment of the Taylor Grazing Act, which granted jurisdiction to Interior, interdepartmental competition continued as Interior lobbied for the National Forests and Agriculture lobbied for the rangelands. The competitive struggle between the two departments appears to have delayed enactment of legislation to control entry and range use from 1920 until 1934, though common property conditions were critical in many parts of the West. This jurisdictional struggle illustrated the significance of bureaucratic goals in determining agency behavior. For bureaucrats seeking to expand budget allocations, jurisdiction over federal land, rather than conservation, was the important issue.

In neither timber land nor rangeland were there significant public good reasons or other externalities to justify land retention by the government. The transfer of property rights to private claimants was lim-

---

[10] See Libecap, "Bureaucratic Opposition."
[11] *Annual Report*, Secretary of the Interior, 1930.

ited through the efforts of the Agriculture and Interior Departments because it was in their bureaucratic interests to do so. Budget appropriations and mandates for land administration depended upon the retention of large tracts of land under government control.

II. *Land Use Decisions under Bureaucratic Administration and Private Property Rights*
A. *Theoretical Predictions*

There are important theoretical reasons for predicting that bureaucratic management will reduce the net contribution of the land resource to social production and wealth. With secure private property rights, long-term decision making regarding investments, harvest practices, and transfers can be made to maximize economic returns. In the absence of significant external effects, private decision makers incur the full social benefits and costs of their actions. Accordingly, decisions to maximize net private returns also maximize net social returns. Moreover, land can be transferred at low cost to other uses whenever higher returns are anticipated. Active markets exist to reduce transaction costs with institutional arrangements for advertising potential sales, for appraising land values, and for securing capital. These conclusions cannot be drawn for bureaucratic management. In addition to the fact that transfers to higher valued uses are more complicated under bureaucratic administration where resource values are often unknown, there are more fundamental reasons for pessimism. First, since bureaucrats do not hold property rights to the land, they do not bear the costs nor receive the benefits of their actions. Thus, they can ignore market signals and engage in socially wasteful land management policies. Second, where use rights or leases for land are assigned to private individuals or firms, the conveyed rights are inherently tenuous because bureaucrats must reallocate land and readjust use privileges to meet changing political conditions. The associated tenure uncertainty encourages short-term, intensive land use practices and discourages long-term investment. Third, because of broad discretionary authority granted agencies by Congress, officials can adopt policies that advance budgets and other bureaucratic goals, even though the policies have negative net social returns. Indeed, most models of self-interest bureaucratic behavior stress the desire of bureaucrats to expand the administrative role, budget, and staff of their agencies. A growing agency provides an environment for advancement to positions of greater authority, salaries, and perquisites. Because of the emphasis on growth, models of bureaucratic behavior predict that bureau output will exceed that which is socially optimal.[12]

---

[12] See Johnson, "Budget Maximization."

B. *Empirical Evidence of the Impact of Bureaucratic Management*

Empirical studies of comparable bureaucratic and private decision making are limited. Nevertheless, the evidence that exists supports the prediction that land values will be lowered under bureaucratic administration. For example, both the Forest Service and the Bureau of Land Management have been criticized for regulating the harvest of timber and range based on biological principles. However, sustained-yield rules are consistent with bureaucratic goals, even though they generally reduce economic returns. Forest Service and BLM officials cannot increase their wealth through optimal harvest strategies, but biological rather than economic criteria for harvesting assist officials in achieving larger budgets. Calculating and monitoring biological conditions requires technically trained staffs and allocations for scientific study. Closely associated to this is an increased agency regulatory role. Ranchers and timber companies have an incentive to avoid agency imposed constraints based on biological criteria, and enforcement of administrative rules is more likely with a technical staff, independent of industry and market conditions. Further, arbitrary biological harvest criteria can be manipulated by officials to meet political pressures. That flexibility, free of profit-maximization requirements, allows the BLM and Forest Service to cultivate supportive client groups for favorable congressional reviews. However, the social costs are likely to be high. Forest Service harvest practices under the sustained-yield constraint result in limited allowable cuts and are tied to silviculture investments. Such investments have had low rates of return. In the Pacific Northwest, where large stands of old-growth timber remain and where harvest costs are relatively low, the Forest Service has strictly limited harvesting. On federal rangeland, the negative results on land values are similar. Conflict between ranchers and BLM personnel for control of the range has led to reduced investment in wells and other improvements. Recent research indicates that efforts by the BLM to meet biological goals through investments in brush removal, plowing, and reseeding have had low returns relative to the opportunity costs of funds.[13] On a broader scale, the BLM is attempting to expand its control over land use through the imposition of allotment management plans over much of the land under its jurisdiction. In some cases, those plans call for stock reductions of 30 percent or more for up to 20 years. The plans are controversial, and besides disrupting established users, they will reduce the net value of the land.

---

[13] See Joe B. Stevens and E. Bruce Godfrey, "Use Rates, Resource Flows, and Efficiency of Public Investment in Range Improvements," *American Journal of Agricultural Economics*, 1972, 54, 611–622.

III. *Concluding Remarks*

The examination of past federal land policies shows that there were no overriding efficiency considerations in retaining the over 700,000,000 acres of land now held by the government. The bureaucratic goals of the Agriculture and the Interior Departments were in conflict with the broad revisions of the land laws necessary to assign property rights in the West. By 1920 both Departments sought to maximize the amount of land under their jurisdictions. Both theory and empirical evidence show that bureaucratic management reduces social land values relative to private decision making under secure rights. Accordingly, there is a clear case for the direct transfer of title. Bureaucratic reforms are not enough. Administrations and laws change, but tenure uncertainty and associated waste continue and can be corrected only through the assignment of definite and secure property rights to the land. The action is necessary to ensure the realization of the potential social contribution of the 740,000,000 acres under federal control.

5

The Federal Estate
by Senator Steven Symms

While this is an impressive gathering of experts in the area of government land acquisition and management, I have mixed emotions about being here. In the 1980 Idaho race for U.S. Senate, my opponent used a television ad against me which showed beautiful Idaho mountain scenery that was fenced off with no trespassing signs. The ad said that if I were elected to the U.S. Senate, Idaho's pristine lands would be sold to the highest bidder. In response, I told Idaho voters that the issue governing the Sagebrush Rebellion was not government ownership vs. private ownership, but federal ownership vs. state ownership. I said that I wanted to transfer some federal lands to the states, and allow the states to use and manage the lands as they saw fit.

Having stated my position, I feel free to speak to you about lands owned by the federal government. By the way, they are government lands, not public lands. They are owned and operated by the federal government, and access is permitted by the government, not the public. Allocation of the resources found on the lands is governed by a federal land manager, not by the marketplace or an unknown "public good." Every day, federal land managers, far removed from the lands they manage, make decisions that adversely affect the livelihoods of those in the private sector.

My philosophy of federal land management always has been one of balance. Federal land management traditionally has not been balanced. It has been caught in the middle of political struggles between private individuals, environmental groups, and government land managers. If properly interpreted and used, the multiple-use concept will balance the most productive uses of federal lands. Sometimes favoring development and sometimes favoring wilderness withdrawal, multiple-use management of government lands could allow lands to be used in a productive, economical, and environmentally sound manner.

But, as with most areas of government, outside influences bias federal practices and pull them further and further from their original intent. Three major trends in land management have resulted from the political struggle surrounding federal land use policies.

Federal land management is, and always will be, economically and environmentally inefficient. The government will never consider maximum efficiency and productivity as essential because government has no competition, no capital charges, and no visible threats to its economic survival. Consequently, government land managers largely ignore the economics of resource and land management. The Forest Service in Idaho, for example, has pursued policies that would eliminate outfitters and guides who run trips on Idaho rivers. It has increased leasing fees on our lakeshores to the point where retirees who have built cabins on their leasehold lands are unsure they can afford to keep them. Idaho forests are full of mature timber that should be harvested, and the land should be reforested. RARE II—the federal government's second attempt to classify wilderness lands—remains unresolved and leaves millions of acres of land in limbo as *de facto* wilderness. Delays continue to plague timber sales because of blanket environmental appeals that do not address *bona fide* issues. Most appeals are filed on the basis of the grey wolf which inhabits the entire North American continent. One was even filed on the basis of the Migratory Bird Treaty Act.

Federal land management inevitably results in elitist land managers who have little or no concern for the problems of those who depend on the land for their livelihood. Far removed from areas their directives affect, the land managers lack sensitivity to local concerns and problems. Federal land managers also lack incentive to be efficient or productive. As Steve Hanke states:

> Government can't act as landlord because government has every incentive to hoard assets. Bureaucrats always hoard assets because they pay no capital carrying charges, or rent, if you will, on the assets that they have. This is precisely why we have the Department of Defense with warehouses full of vacuum tubes from 1935 shortwave radio sets. It costs the Defense Department zero to carry those assets rather than to liquidate them and put the capital to more productive use.

The federal government has grown tremendously over the past few decades. In the area of federal lands, more attention has been given to land acquisition than to the careful and productive management of existing holdings. The increase of the federal estate becomes critical as statistics show that most of our valuable resources are on federal lands. Eighty-five percent of our estimated oil reserves, 72 percent of the oil shale, 37 percent of the natural gas, and over 50 percent of our mineral deposits are located on federal lands. As we attempt to end our dependence on foreign sources of strategic resources, we need increased exploration and development of domestic resources. But many of the federal areas that contain important strategic resources are closed to development and exploration, and others are enmeshed in governmental red tape.

Because the federal government will always consider itself the best land manager, nothing short of ownership of the land will be sufficient to meet federal land policy objectives. As I noted earlier, I am not a proponent of the sale of federal lands to private interests except in certain circumstances. But the federal government needs to reform its land management. It is simply good management practice to evaluate assets continually to determine whether or not they are still serving their best good. This is true even when the best good is a public good.

The Administration has begun to advocate the disposal of some surplus federal lands. The proposals for federal land disposal have been modest: of the almost 700 million acres of federal land, the Administration wants to sell only one million. Senator Percy has also furthered the cause of efficient land use and management by introducing a bill in Congress which would ask that current assets of the federal government be appraised and that the unnecessary properties be sold. Of course, parks, monuments, historic sights, wilderness areas, wildlife refuges, and other protected areas would be exempt from sale and would remain under government control. While I support the transfer of some wilderness areas from federal to state control, I also think that surplus lands covered in Senator Percy's resolution should be sold to private individuals and groups. Certainly, in view of a $115 billion federal deficit, the federal government must stop thinking that it must own everything.

Although it has been misconstrued and overstated by its opponents, President Reagan's good neighbor policy is clearly a step in the right direction. The good neighbor policy involves the transfer of land to the states at less than the fair market value if states request such a transfer. The Administration, and Secretary Watt in particular, is undertaking a careful land stewardship policy. In land acquisition, they buy only as much land as is needed to carry out the federal resource goals, and they sell excess and certain other types of federal lands. This is not a wholesale auction. It is a sale of a small percentage of the property which falls into specific categories: land, near cities and towns, which constricts urban development; scattered nonurban lands, which are often checkerboard lands and are inefficient to manage; and lands which should be agricultural, commercial, or industrial. The policy protects parks, national wildlife refuges, Indian trust lands, wilderness areas, wild and scenic rivers, national trails, conservation areas, recreation areas, and other congressionally designated areas. The policy will not weaken any resources protection, it will not close any access to hunters, fishermen, or recreational people, and it will not disrupt real estate markets and values. But if a portion of the West were opened up for privatization, opportunities would develop for people to start new entrepreneurial activities.

I do not foresee insoluble problems with transfer of some federal lands to states and private parties, but many people fear such transfers. Often people want to trim the federal government, but they do not want to pay anybody for the use of what are now federal lands. They do not want to pay a fee to go hunting, pay more for the production of timber, or pay more for any use of the land.

Underlying this issue is the question of government ownership and government control versus management through the market system where free men, working through free institutions, allocate scarce resources. It is senseless to lock up valuable minerals and resources that this country will need and to forbid development of critical resources. We must make some drastic changes in U.S. land and resources management. I certainly welcome this conference and thank The Heritage Foundation for focusing some light on this critical subject.

6

Energy Resources
by M. Bruce Johnson

There is little doubt that the United States has both generous quantities and wide varieties of energy resources. Some estimates suggest that we are endowed with sufficient amounts of crude oil, natural gas liquids, natural gas, coal, uranium, shale oil, and tar sands to produce more energy in the future than we have in the past, dating back to the time when we began to extract and use these substances. The tables included in the Appendix to this paper trace the time path of "proved reserves" from 1950 through 1979 for crude oil, natural gas, and coal. The story that emerges from these numbers should be well-known to everyone. Proved reserves have increased slightly over this thirty-year period; domestic production of coal and crude oil has increased by approximately 50 percent and domestic production of natural gas has risen by 200 percent. On the other hand, consumption of natural gas and crude oil has increased at a far more rapid rate. Coal lags for a variety of reasons. The difference between domestic consumption and production, of course, is made up by imports, which tend to come from politically and economically unstable and insecure sources.

Proponents of the natural resources "doomsday" hypothesis occasionally calculate the number of years of a resource still available if current rates of consumption continue into the future. This involves simply dividing current consumption into the proved reserves for a particular energy resource. Such an analysis for the period from 1950 to 1979 indicates that the number of remaining years of proved resources has declined for all categories of energy resources.

If we divide crude reserves by annual domestic consumption for each year, natural gas declines from 32 years to just under 10 years worth of reserves and crude oil declines from 11 years to 4 years. Simple computations of this type, however, are more likely to be misleading than informative; the economic implications of the result must be handled with great care. Obviously, the calculations depend on the accuracy of the underlying estimates. Suffice it to say that the U.S. Geological Survey has an uncertain record of forecasting energy reserves. In 1885, the survey saw "little or no chance for oil in California." In 1891, the same forecast was made for the states of Kansas and Texas. By 1908, the Geological Survey estimated a maximum future supply of oil that has been exceeded long ago. On the other hand, the American Gas Association predicted only a few years ago that the U.S. had enough gas to last from 1000 to 2500 years at current consumption rates. Dr. Vincent E. McKelvey, with 37 years experience at the U.S. Geological Survey, including six years as Director, stated in 1977 that "as much as...3000 to 4000 times the amount of natural gas the United States will consume... will be sealed in the geo-pressured zones underlying the Gulf coast region." Unfortunately, that optimistic forecast cost Mr. McKelvey his position as Director of the Survey. Perhaps the lesson is that forecasting potential energy reserves is scientifically and politically risky.

While we have fewer years' worth of proved resources today than we had in 1950, it is not a meaningful constraint on our energy future. Consider, for example, the case of crude oil in 1979. From society's point of view the numbers indicate we had four years' worth of domestic reserves if we were to service all of our domestic consumption from domestic proved reserves. Suppose, in 1979, an investor contemplated the expenditure of $30 to acquire a barrel of crude oil at the then current prices. Alternatively, that $30 could have been invested in exploration to prove up new reserves. Given that we already had four years' worth of reserves, a new barrel added to proved reserves would be a marginal barrel available for production or sale four years hence. Certainly the passage of those four years involved an opportunity cost represented, perhaps, by the Moody's Triple A corporate bond rate which stood at 9.63 percent in 1979.

Calculations show that the future value four years hence of a barrel of crude would have to have an anticipated value of $43.80 in order to make it worthwhile to invest in exploration for additional crude. At today's interest rate of 15 percent, a prudent investor would have to expect at least $53 a barrel for crude four years hence in order to make an addition to proved reserves worthwhile. Conversely, if one expected the price of crude to be $43.80 four years hence, one could afford to invest no more than $24.70 today in exploration costs at a 15 percent discount rate. Finally, $30 spent today for a new barrel 10 years hence requires an expected price of $121 at 15 percent.

Prudent investors and managers, whose personal and corporate wealth and careers are at stake, will respond to current and expected future prices and interest rates in a rational and socially beneficial fashion. This assumes, of course, that markets are allowed to exist and function. In fact, the tremendous potential for the timely discovery and development of domestic energy resources has been crippled and distorted by both our institutions and the policies governing the management of public lands.

Energy Resources Potential of Federal Lands

The U.S. Geological Survey has estimated that the United States can expect to produce approximately 164 billion barrels of crude oil and natural gas liquids in the future and that, conservatively, 37 percent of the nation's undiscovered crude oil and 43 percent of its undiscovered natural gas are on federal lands. The Department of the Interior has estimated 40 percent of the demonstrated coal reserves and 80 percent of the recoverable oil shale reserves are also on federal lands. Table 4 in the Appendix shows that federal lands currently are contributing far less than their *pro rata* share of energy resources production. For example, while an estimated 37 percent of undiscovered crude oil resides on government lands, only 14 percent of current U.S. production comes from government lands. Clearly the complicated tangle of federal acts and administrative directives and stipulations have hindered production of energy resources on federal lands. There are more than 60 federal acts affecting the use of public lands, ranging from the 1862 Homestead Act to the 1980 Alaskan National Interest Lands Conservation Act. Administrative stipulations and regulations number in the hundreds.

The effect of these statutes and rules is to increase the time involved in development, to increase the costs of energy, and to reduce the amount of energy resources produced. For example, the amended OCS Lands Act requires that the Secretary of the Interior call for information on leasable areas, perform a tentative track selection, draft an Environmental Impact Statement (EIS), produce a final EIS, give public notice of a proposed sale, receive and review the comments from the coastal states affected, issue a notice of sale, and evaluate the received bids. This pre-leasing process may take two-and-a-half to three-and-a-half years. The opportunity cost to U.S. energy consumers is substantial, and the otherwise avoidable cost to the bidders must be reflected in lower bonus payments to the government in a world where crude oil prices are determined in an international market.

As wasteful and inefficient as current leasing practices are, they shrink in significance when compared to locking up vast areas of federal lands. Congress passed the Wilderness Act of 1964 and created the National Wilderness Preservation System (NWPS). Although that act contained a provision for the leasing of oil, gas, and other mineral rights for 20 years, few leases have been issued. Of those granted, the operating conditions imposed were so severe as to render exploration and development virtually impossible. No new oil or natural gas leases can be issued after December 31, 1983. Consequently, much of the wilderness area of the United States remains unexplored and its energy and mineral resource reserves remain unknown. The lost potential is enormous: in 1964, 15 million acres were involved. By 1981, the NWPS contained nearly 78 million acres. When current reviews are completed, the total could reach 118 million acres.

The logic of this lockup is baffling. Proponents of federal ownership and management of lands have argued that such government decision making is superior to private decision making because of the former's rationality, logic, and foresight. But if rational decision making requires knowledge, how can the lockup policy be justified? How can rational and well-informed decisions on resource allocation and development be made if the decision makers are foreclosed from acquiring the very knowledge necessary for such decisions?

National security is a valid reason for holding inventories of energy resources. Yet, the current lockup policies cannot be justified on those grounds either. Rational management of strategic energy reserves requires knowledge of the resource base so that security considerations can be assessed against potential environmental costs. But without hard information, environmental groups prevail by default.

If someone owned a parcel of land fee simple as a private investor, he could refrain voluntarily from informing himself about the characteristics and potential of that land. In so doing, he would individually bear the opportunity cost of his ignorance. When this practice is followed on public lands, neither Congress nor the bureaucrats bear the cost. Instead, consumers and taxpayers shoulder the burden through higher energy prices and higher taxes. The costs of the contrived ignorance is shifted from those responsible for informed, intelligent decision making to those for whom the land is theoretically held in trust.

Obviously, the alleged "beneficiaries" of this trust are numerous, diffuse in their interests, uninformed, and unorganized. They can be, and have been, ignored by the congressional and bureaucratic stewards of public lands. Instead, public lands decision makers have devoted themselves exclusively to balancing their two main special interest constituencies: energy producers and the environmentalists. U.S. policy with respect to government lands has been an unequal balance between the interests of energy producers and organized environmental groups. The interests of consumers and taxpayers largely have been ignored.

Special Interest Group Incentives

Organized environmental groups have a clear interest in suppressing or preventing the acquisition of information and knowledge about energy resources on public lands. Although this is not an end in itself, it is a means to promoting their goal of adding to the inventory of wilderness and undeveloped public lands. Consider two alternative scenarios: first, suppose we have a tract of public land unambiguously known to have extensive deposits of energy resources. Second, consider another tract identical to the first except that there is no reliable information about its energy resource endowments. Given two such tracts, differing only in the amount of information about the energy characteristics of one tract and given limited resources and rational behavior on the part of energy producing companies, political pressure for energy development will be focused on the first tract, with its known potential. Furthermore, no individual energy producer would have the incentive to invest in information production for the second tract because of the public good nature of such information; under the current property rights structure—or lack thereof—the benefits of producing such information will not be captured by the firm that incurs the cost. Traditionally, economic analysis has suggested that government has a role in producing such information precisely because of the public-good aspects. However, it is clear the government has failed to perform this role in connection with vast reaches of government land under its control.

Against the background of secularly declining energy prices in every category, Congress responded to the 1973 energy crisis by installing price and allocation controls, passing some twenty federal acts restricting the use of public lands, and imposing windfall profits taxes on producers. These are simply the three most important general categories; in fact, the result was the creation of a regulatory labyrinth so involved, arbitrary, and uncertain that no human being is capable of describing, let alone appreciating, the full implications of the conglomeration of energy laws and regulations implemented during the past decade. Yet the net result is clear: each provision of our energy policy has raised the cost of energy production and discouraged productive activity. In other words, the secular decline in energy prices would have suffered a brief reversal in the mid-70s except for our short-run, politically motivated policy response. Instead of encouraging exploration and development of energy resources, we imposed taxes, regulations, and other constraints on the very activities and entities that could have led to larger supplies and lower prices for consumers.

The Depoliticization of Energy

There are few real possibilities for reform of government energy policies as long as the issue remains politicized. Consumers and taxpayers are not well organized and invariably will lose if resource decisions remain in the hands of a Congress and a bureaucracy inclined to satisfy organized special interest groups. The efficient management of resources is impossible if the decision process is loaded against development. Increasingly, exploration and development requires unanimity among every special interest group while inaction requires only one dissenting party in the political gauntlet any current project must run.

Partial depoliticization of energy could be accomplished by the establishment of private property rights. At the very least, this would re-

47

dress the balance between those forces opposed to development and those in favor. Under a system of private property rights, land and resource owners have the incentive to become informed about the potential value of their holdings and to become informed at their own expense. The quality of information available should improve dramatically, and the consequences of good and bad investment would be decentralized and placed in the private sector.

The widely recognized efficiencies of a private property system are not guaranteed unless the property rights regime is stable. If private property rights in land are subject to the uncertainty of arbitrary regulations and expropriation, the time horizons of private owners collapse commensurately. Considering the land use regulations currently promulgated by every city and hamlet (with the exception of Houston), it is difficult to believe that the privatization of energy resources and government lands will be an unambiguous success. Yet, such privatization is clearly a step in the direction of establishing more efficient resource allocation through improved incentives. Whether government held land is auctioned off, or simply given away, is of far less consequence in the long run than the improved efficiencies that will surely result. Whether disbursed by auction, lottery, or grant, titles to federal lands will be traded quickly in a private market. Property rights should be auctioned off to provide some assistance with federal budgets. However, the long-run efficiency gains in resource use far outweigh the short-term proceeds from such a sale. Perhaps in the interest of solving another contemporary problem, potential social security recipients could be offered parcels of land in return for their voluntary withdrawal from the social security system.

The real cost of energy declined during the century in which we have recorded data. That trend could resume and contribute to continued improvements in our standard of living if we restructure our institutions in such a way as to unleash the creativity, vitality, and risk taking of our citizens. The reestablishment of private property rights and land is the greatest hope and best investment available to us.

Table 1
Crude Oil (U.S. Domestic/Billion Barrels)

Year	Proved Reserves	Domestic Production	Domestic Consumption	Years "Supply"	Years "Demand"
1950	25.30	1.97	2.36	12.82	10.73
1951	27.50	2.25	2.56	12.23	10.74
1952	28.00	2.29	2.66	12.23	10.52
1953	28.90	2.36	2.77	12.26	10.42
1954	29.60	2.32	2.83	12.79	10.46
1955	30.00	2.48	3.09	12.08	9.72
1956	30.40	2.62	3.21	11.62	9.46
1957	30.30	2.62	3.22	11.58	9.42
1958	30.50	2.45	3.33	12.45	9.16
1959	31.70	2.58	3.48	12.31	9.12
1960	31.60	2.58	3.59	12.27	8.81
1961	31.80	2.62	3.64	12.13	8.73
1962	31.40	2.68	3.80	11.73	8.27
1963	31.00	2.75	3.92	11.26	7.91
1964	31.00	2.79	4.03	11.12	7.68
1965	31.40	2.85	4.20	11.02	7.47
1966	31.50	3.03	4.41	10.40	7.14
1967	31.40	3.22	4.59	9.76	6.85
1968	30.70	3.33	4.90	9.22	6.26
1969	29.60	3.37	5.16	8.78	5.74
1970	39.00	3.52	5.36	11.09	7.27
1971	38.10	3.45	5.55	11.03	6.86
1972	36.30	3.46	5.99	10.51	6.06
1973	35.30	3.36	6.32	10.50	5.59
1974	34.20	3.20	6.08	10.68	5.63
1975	32.70	3.06	5.96	10.70	5.49
1976	30.90	2.98	6.39	10.38	4.83
1977	29.50	3.01	6.73	9.80	4.39
1978	27.80	3.18	6.88	8.75	4.04
1979	27.10	3.12	6.76	8.68	4.01

Proved Reserves are from Table 19 of the 1980 Annual Report to Congress Volume Two: Data; Energy Information Administration, Department of Energy.

Domestic Production is from Table 2 of the 1980 Annual Report to Congress Volume Two: Data; Energy Information Administration, Department of Energy.

Domestic Consumption is from Table 3 of the 1980 Annual Report to Congress Volume Two: Data; Energy Information Administration, Department of Energy.

Years Supply is Proved Reserves/Domestic Production.

Years Demand is Proved Reserves/Domestic Consumption.

Table 2
Natural Gas (U.S. Domestic/Trillion Cubic Feet)

Year	Proved Reserves	Domestic Production	Domestic Consumption	Years "Supply"	Years "Demand"
1950	184.60	6.02	5.77	30.66	31.99
1951	192.80	7.16	6.81	26.93	28.31
1952	198.60	7.69	7.29	25.83	27.24
1953	210.30	8.06	7.64	26.09	27.53
1954	210.60	8.39	8.05	25.10	26.16
1955	222.50	9.03	8.69	24.64	25.60
1956	236.50	9.66	9.29	24.48	25.46
1957	245.20	10.25	9.85	23.92	24.89
1958	252.80	10.57	10.30	23.92	24.54
1959	261.20	11.55	11.32	22.61	23.07
1960	262.30	12.23	11.97	21.45	21.91
1961	266.30	12.66	12.49	21.03	21.32
1962	272.30	13.25	13.27	20.55	20.52
1963	276.20	14.08	13.97	19.62	19.77
1964	281.30	14.82	14.81	18.98	18.99
1965	286.50	15.29	15.28	18.74	18.75
1966	289.30	16.47	16.45	17.57	17.59
1967	292.90	17.39	17.39	16.84	16.84
1968	287.30	18.49	18.63	15.54	15.42
1969	275.10	19.83	20.06	13.87	13.71
1970	290.70	21.01	21.14	13.84	13.75
1971	278.80	21.61	21.79	12.90	12.79
1972	266.10	21.62	22.10	12.31	12.04
1973	250.00	21.73	22.05	11.50	11.34
1974	237.10	20.71	21.22	11.45	11.17
1975	228.00	19.24	19.54	11.85	11.67
1976	216.00	19.10	19.95	11.31	10.83
1977	208.90	19.16	19.52	10.90	10.70
1978	200.30	19.12	19.63	10.48	10.20
1979	194.90	19.66	20.24	9.91	9.63

Proved Reserves are from Table 19 of the 1980 Annual Report to Congress Volume Two: Data; Energy Information Administration, Department of Energy.

Domestic Production is from Table 2 of the 1980 Annual Report to Congress Volume Two: Data; Energy Information Administration, Department of Energy.

Domestic Consumption is from Table 3 of the 1980 Annual Report to Congress Volume Two: Data; Energy Information Administration, Department of Energy.

Years Supply is Proved Reserves/Domestic Production.

Years Demand is Proved Reserves/Domestic Consumption.

Table 3
Coal (U.S. Domestic/Billion Short Tons)

Year	Proved Reserves	Domestic Production	Domestic Consumption	Years "Supply"	Years "Demand"
1950	N.A.	0.56	0.49	N.A.	N.A.
1951	N.A.	0.58	0.51	N.A.	N.A.
1952	N.A.	0.51	0.55	N.A.	N.A.
1953	N.A.	0.49	0.45	N.A.	N.A.
1954	N.A.	0.42	0.39	N.A.	N.A.
1955	N.A.	0.49	0.45	N.A.	N.A.
1956	N.A.	0.53	0.46	N.A.	N.A.
1957	N.A.	0.52	0.43	N.A.	N.A.
1958	N.A.	0.43	0.39	N.A.	N.A.
1959	N.A.	0.43	0.39	N.A.	N.A.
1960	N.A.	0.43	0.40	N.A.	N.A.
1961	N.A.	0.42	0.39	N.A.	N.A.
1962	N.A.	0.44	0.40	N.A.	N.A.
1963	N.A.	0.48	0.42	N.A.	N.A.
1964	N.A.	0.50	0.45	N.A.	N.A.
1965	N.A.	0.53	0.47	N.A.	N.A.
1966	N.A.	0.55	0.50	N.A.	N.A.
1967	N.A.	0.56	0.49	N.A.	N.A.
1968	N.A.	0.56	0.51	N.A.	N.A.
1969	N.A.	0.57	0.52	N.A.	N.A.
1970	N.A.	0.61	0.52	N.A.	N.A.
1971	N.A.	0.56	0.50	N.A.	N.A.
1972	N.A.	0.60	0.52	N.A.	N.A.
1973	136.71	0.60	0.56	228.39	243.00
1974	N.A.	0.61	0.56	N.A.	N.A.
1975	N.A.	0.65	0.56	N.A.	N.A.
1976	N.A.	0.68	0.60	N.A.	N.A.
1977	N.A.	0.70	0.63	N.A.	N.A.
1978	474.56	0.67	0.63	708.08	759.05
1979	0.00	0.78	0.68	0.00	0.00

1973 Proved Reserves from Table 4 of Demonstrated Coal Reserve Base of the United States on January 1, 1974; Mineral Industry Surveys, U.S. Dept. of the Interior.

1978 Proved Reserves from Table 3 of Demonstrated Coal Reserve in the United States on January 1, 1979; U.S. Dept. of Energy. Energy Information Administration

Domestic Production is from Table 2 of the 1980 Annual Report to Congress Volume Two: Data; Energy Information Administration, Department of Energy.

Domestic Consumption is from Table 3 of the 1980 Annual Report to Congress Volume Two: Data; Energy Information Administration, Department of Energy.

Years Supply is Proved Reserves/Domestic Production.

Years Demand is Proved Reserves/Domestic Consumption.

Table 4
Estimated Potential and Production of
Energy Resources from Government Lands

Energy Resources	Estimated Percent on Government Lands	Percent of Current U.S. Production from Government Lands
Undiscovered Crude Oil	37	14
Undiscovered Natural Gas	43	28
Remaining Coal Resources	40	8
Recoverable Oil Shale	80	*
Tar Sands	75	*
Uranium Ore (U_3O_8)**	32	39

*Current U.S. Production negligible.
**Estimated recoverable at $50 per pound.
Sources: U.S. Department of the Interior, Department of Energy, Federal Trade Commission.

7

Privatizing Wilderness Lands: The Political Economy of Harmony and Good Will

by John Baden

Wilderness has a high, though not infinite, social value. As such, development or conversion imply a cost. In those rare instances when welfare would be enhanced by developing wilderness areas, any development not designed to lessen the negative impact on pristine quality is inefficient. For the purposes of this paper, wilderness is defined as lands so classified under the 1964 Act or those lands that are eligible for such classification.

Since the obvious geographical areas have already been classified as wilderness, advocates have relaxed their standards and are now promoting formerly logged, roaded, mined, and otherwise developed areas as prime candidates for inclusion in the wilderness system. While it may be condemned as hypocritical, this new emphasis has uncovered a formerly unacceptable fact: development can be reversible. In parts of the Southeast, for example, the skills of a trained forest ecologist are required to determine whether an apparently pristine area is actually in a stage of recovery from logging, farming, or roading. To the casual observer and even the dedicated backpacker, the scars are invisible. This is encouraging evidence of the land's ability to recover.

In view of current and projected economic conditions and technological potentialities, it seems obvious that the overwhelming majority of wilderness lands are most valuable when maintained as wilderness. This can be explained in terms of opportunity costs. To economists and political econmists, all costs are opportunity costs; that is, the highest valued alternative sacrificed because of an action. This is known also as the alternative cost doctrine. The cost of logging or otherwise desecrating the Lincoln-Scapegoat Wilderness in Montana, for example, includes the private costs associated with development—such as labor, machinery, diesel fuel, maintenance, and the cost of capital—and the values of the wilderness experiences foregone if the forest is clearcut and the drainage system is modified by a parallel road system. Even though the value of the land as wilderness may be high, it is not infinite.

In this case, however, the opportunity costs of preserving the Lincoln-Scapegoat are far lower than the costs of developing it. This and hundreds of other examples have demonstrated the need to put wilderness areas in private hands.

Privatizing Wilderness

Although many arguments can be used to support the privatization of wilderness lands, the most important one is simple: there are good reasons to believe that over the long run the government cannot be trusted to behave in an ecologically sensitive, efficient, equitable, and farsighted manner. The arguments supporting this claim are presented below. First, it is useful to review some of the history of America's public lands.

The founding fathers strongly believed that government should not own the means of production. Because of their exposure to European history and their recent experience with British control, their conviction that land should be owned by private parties became an important philosophical component of the American Revolution and the Constitution that developed from it. The first one hundred years of the U.S. political experiment, from the Northwest Ordinance through the various homestead and preemption acts, applied this principle as land was transferred to private parties.

Such transfers were a mixed blessing, bringing us the counter-revolution of the progressive era. The counter-revolution was predicated on the assumption that private parties are incapable of managing natural resources. To the proponents of public ownership, management, and control, overwhelmingly strong arguments supported their position. There was ample evidence of environmental pillage and plunder, graft and corruption, and a lack of environmental stewardship. Unfortunately, the progressives failed to observe two fundamental facts.

First, many problems that occurred on the public lands were a result of the failure to define and enforce property rights to resources. Common property resources included fish, buffalo, and waterways—fugitive resources all—but they also included much public grass and timber land. In the absence of well-defined and enforced property rights to a resource, overexploitation can be expected. This institutional failure can be remedied by establishing appropriate institutions.[1]

Second, the advocates of public ownership failed to understand that it does not make sense privately or socially to economize on resources

---

[1] For a discussion of the development of property rights, see Harold Demsetz, "Toward a Theory of Property Rights," *American Economic Review* (May 1967); R. N. Johnson, M. Gisser, and M. Werner, "The Definition of a Surface Water Right and Transfer Ability," *Journal of Law and Economics* (October 1981); Terry L. Anderson and P. J.

with relatively low value. When capital and labor are dear but land and associated resources are cheap and plentiful, it is privately and socially rational to conserve what is dear and squander what is cheap. Today's efficient forestry and milling practices would have been ill-advised a century ago, even if they had been technically possible. When timber had a low or even negative value, it was handled in a manner that reflected its value, but when standing timber sells for several hundred dollars per thousand board feet, as it does today, efforts are made to economize on its use.[2]

Because the progressive observers of the late 1800s did not appreciate the constraints and opportunities faced by decision makers in the system, they initiated a counter-revolution whose costs and benefits we face today. A counter-counter-revolution—perhaps as a tribute to the bicentennial of the Constitution—should be initiated, calling for the privatization of wilderness lands which will lead to greater ecological sensitivity in their management and more economic efficiency, equity, and foresightedness in their administration. While some of these claims may appear counter-intuitive, the following discussion should provide a convincing rationale.

Environmental Sensitivity

If one holds the optimistic conviction that wilderness areas are forever inviolate, managing people becomes the only relevant issue. Even if the extraction of strategic minerals, oil pools, and gas deposits were not an issue in the management of wilderness lands—as they increasingly are—the problem of people remains. Wilderness is being loved to death. Since the demand for wilderness seems to increase with increments in wealth and education and since wilderness recreation is not taxed, it is reasonable to anticipate that pressure will increase on wilderness areas. This is a larger problem than most people realize.

In an effort to limit the negative effects of recreationists on wilderness lands, the Forest Service has initiated rationing systems to control access and use.[3] If congestion and queuing for access increase signifi-

---

Hill, "From Free Grass to Fences: Transforming the Commons of the American West," in *Managing the Commons*, ed. Garrett Hardin and John Baden (San Francisco: W. H. Freeman, 1977), pp. 200–216; and John Umbeck, "A Theory of Contract Choice in the California Gold Rush," *Journal of Law and Economics* (October 1977).

[2] For a discussion of conservation practices in forestry, see John Baden and Richard Stroup, "Entrepreneurship, Energy, and the Political Economy of Hope," in *Proceedings of the Southwestern Legal Foundation: Exploration and Economics of the Petroleum Industry*, vol. 19 (New York: Matthew Bender, 1981), pp. 337–360; and *idem*, "Political Economy Perspectives on the Sagebrush Rebellion," *Public Land Law Review* 3 (July 1982).

[3] George H. Stankey and John Baden, "Rationing Wilderness Use: Methods, Problems and Guidelines," Research Paper INT-192 (Ogden, Utah: Forest Service, Intermountain Forest and Range Experiment Station, July 1977).

cantly, political pressure and lobbying likely will be used in attempts to change wilderness management standards.[4] Perhaps the well-educated elite will be able to use the political process to retain current standards; but wilderness areas are publicly owned, and many other groups may successfully gain access through relentless political pressure, leading to a gradual reduction in environmental quality. A privately managed wilderness system dominated by purists and managed under a system of binding covenants would not confront the same political pressures.

There are other, potentially more serious pressures that may be exerted on the government to alter the management and character of wilderness lands. Most educated Americans are aware that a shortage of strategic minerals could be serious. As the name suggests, these minerals are believed to be critical to a technologically advanced society, and a shortage could devastate the U.S. economy and compromise national security. Senator Harrison Schmitt (R.-N.Mex.) states: "We have sufficient understanding of the broad technology base necessary to develop, in the next 50 to 100 years, renewable energy sources of various kinds; but when you look at the strategic minerals on which we are dependent, on foreign imports from unstable and unfriendly areas of the world, we have few alternatives to find."[5]

The opportunity costs of failing to develop a cobalt mine in a wilderness area, for example, would increase dramatically if foreign sources of cobalt were cut off. Unlike the Soviet Union, which is self-sufficient in cobalt, the United States imports 97 percent of its net consumption from politically unstable and sometimes hostile countries. Senator Schmitt speaks to the issue of developing federal lands and easing environmental standards to develop strategic minerals: "The encouraging thing I find in Secretary Watt's philosophy is that we can manage public lands for the protection of those lands and for the enjoyment of future generations, as well as provide adequate development in the national interests. We have to be willing to do both."[6] But the fact remains that not all good things go together. Some trade-offs are inherent in the production of recreational amenities and cobalt in wilderness areas; roads, mines, and tailings will always conflict with preserving pristine wilderness.

If national security considerations mandated the development of a cobalt mine in a wilderness area, who would an environmentalist prefer to manage that development—James Watt, Secretary of Interior, or Russell Peterson, President of the Audubon Society? Although a land apart, wilderness is also a part of a larger political and economic system, and

<hr>

[4] John Baden, "Neospartan Hedonists, Adult Toy Aficionados, and the Rationing of Public Lands," in *Managing the Commons*, pp. 241-251.

[5] Council on Economics and National Security (CENS), *Strategic Minerals: A Resource Crisis* (Washington, D.C.: CENS, 1981), p. 75.

[6] *Ibid.*, p. 81.

one can easily imagine situations in which a mineral or energy resource would be developed in a wilderness area. The ecological sensitivity displayed is a function of the information and incentives faced by those who are responsible for managing the development. Inflamed by the consequences of a cutoff of a strategic mineral, Congress could remove the wilderness status of an area; but it would be more constrained in dealings with private lands. Furthermore, the incentives faced by a leader of the Audubon Society are quite different than those confronted by the Secretary of Interior.

If a nonprofit, private environmental group were to manage development on wilderness lands, it would face strong incentives to match incentives to preserve with demands for strategic minerals. Potentials for innovation should not be underestimated when private parties confront trade-offs. An outstanding example is the way the Audubon Society imaginatively and rationally monitors the development of its petroleum properties on its Rainey Preserve. In such operations, costs are reduced and everyone wins.

Our recent book, *Bureaucracy vs. Environment: The Environmental Costs of Bureaucratic Governance*, graphically recounts how federal agencies are often insensitive to environmental values.[7] Despite reasonable intentions, the bureaucratic entrepreneurs of the Forest Service, the Bureau of Land Management, the Bureau of Reclamation, the Army Corps of Engineers, and the Bureau of Indian Affairs consistently and systematically have used the federal treasury to subsidize the destruction of environmental quality. There is little reason to believe that this pattern will change should wilderness areas be developed because of a strategic minerals or energy embargo.

The Forest Service, which controls 187 million acres of public land, was established in 1905 to bring scientific, businesslike management to the federal forests. While it has employed science, it consistently has shown little regard for economy or efficiency as it has systematically mismanaged vast tracts of forest and wilderness land. For example, the agency has terraced portions of our national forests in efforts to produce more timber, planned recreational developments in wilderness areas, and managed deficit timber sales. As William Hyde notes, "multiple use requirements, restrictions on clear cutting..., and high logging road standards all increase harvest costs on the...public lands.... Together these factors have made forest management, especially forest management on public lands, one of the more controversial areas in all resource and environmental management."[8] The Forest Service has

---

[7] John Baden and Richard L. Stroup, eds., *Bureaucracy vs. Environment: The Environmental Costs of Bureaucratic Governance* (Ann Arbor: University of Michigan Press, 1981).

[8] William Hyde, *Timber Supply, Land Allocation, and Economic Efficiency* (Baltimore: Johns Hopkins University Press, 1980).

managed to road and log forests that are *de facto* wilderness areas, using techniques that would fail the cost versus revenue calculations of private timber companies.[9]

The BLM's record is even more discouraging. The agency has chained millions of acres of pinyon-juniper ecosystems in the "Elfin Forests" in the Southwest and has designed controversial rest rotation programs for use on 87 percent of its grazing areas.[10] Another agency, the Bureau of Reclamation, destroyed winter range by building the Teton Dam and other economically inefficient projects justified only at 3, 4, or 5 percent interest rates, while ignoring the negative externalities (those costs that accrue to parties other than the decision maker) imposed by these projects.[11] The Bureau of Indian Affairs outlawed traditional checks on overgrazing, fostering the development of the worst range conditions ever experienced in the United States and impoverishing Indians in the name of communal ownership.[12] The Army Corps of Engineers attempted to justify the expansion of its activities by referring to an energy crisis generated largely by governmental policies.[13]

Efficiency

Unfortunately, bureaucratic managers are largely insulated from the consequences of their decisions. With well-defined, enforceable property rights, however, the linkage of authority with responsibility is fostered, and the incentives for individual decision makers are determined by the rules of the game. The decision maker in a private organization is rewarded when he successfully carries out entrepreneurial activities. He becomes a residual claimant with property rights in the residuals that are generated by increased resource allocation. This system gives the manager the incentive to monitor input use, since improved efficiency will increase his reward. As a result, efficiency is enhanced. In this institutional arrangement, private actors suffer the consequences and gain the benefits of their actions. There is no analogous mechanism within federal agencies, but this is not the fault of bad people. It is the fault of poor institutional design.

---

[9] See Barney Dowdle, "An Institutional Dinosaur with an Ace: Or, How to Piddle Away Public Timber Wealth and Foul the Environment in the Process," in *Bureaucracy vs. Environment*, pp. 170–185; and Marion Clawson, "The National Forests," *Science* 191 (1976), pp. 762–767.

[10] See Sabine Kremp, "A Perspective on BLM Grazing Policy," in *Bureaucracy vs. Environment*, pp. 124–53, and Bernard Shanks, "Dams and Disasters: The Social Problems of Water Development Policies," in *ibid.*, pp. 108–123.

[11] See Gary Libecap and Ronald N. Johnson, "The Navajo and Too Many Sheep," in *ibid.*, pp. 87–107.

[12] See Shanks, "Dams and Disasters."

[13] Thomas Sowell, *Knowledge & Decisions* (New York: Basic Books, 1980), esp. pp. 122–126.

Unnecessarily squandering wilderness resources is inefficient. Although the nonprofit status of environmental groups significantly weakens the incentives inherent in residual claimacy, the literature clearly indicates that the managers of nonprofit organizations often capture a portion of the rents gained from enhanced efficiency.[14] To the degree that managers succeed in expropriating rents, they will encourage their organizations to behave efficiently.

Private Ownership and Equitable Management

George Bernard Shaw's dictum that any policy that robs Peter to pay Paul will enjoy Paul's support is a fundamental principle of political economy. Supporters of wilderness classification have been using the governmental apparatus as an engine of plunder.[15] Surveys of the demographic basis of support for environmental quality in general and wilderness in particular consistently demonstrate that these advocates are not disadvantaged citizens. As the advertisements in *Audubon Magazine* suggest, membership in such organizations is correlated positively with high income and education. Since wealth and political power are correlated positively in all systems, it should come as no surprise that concern for amenity and wilderness preservation is not monopolized by the activist liberal crowd satirized by Tom Wolfe. A recent study found that "support for private property rights, laissez-faire government, and economic growth [is] strongly correlated with environmental concern, and explain[s] far more variation in the latter than do the demographic variables. . . ."[16]

To the degree that wilderness classification reduces the supply of timber, minerals, energy, and agricultural products, wealth is transferred from the general consumer to the person who appreciates wilderness. In most wilderness areas, this loss is trivial or nonexistent. Wilderness classification often saves the taxpayer money, since it precludes the active manipulations of bureaucratic entrepreneurs in federal agencies. Yet, the degree to which wealth transfers are imposed by wilderness classification tends to be highly regressive. There is also the somewhat

---

[14] Jensen and Meckling, "Theory of the Firm: Managerial Behavior, Agency Costs, and Ownership Structure," *Journal of Financial Economy* (1976); and Alchian and Demsetz, "Production, Information Costs, and Economic Organization," *Economic Review* (December 1972).

[15] For a more extended discussion, see John Baden, Randy Simmons, and Rodney D. Fort, "Environmentalists and Self-Interest: How Pure Are Those Who Desire the Pristine?" in *Earth Day Reconsidered*, ed. John Baden (Washington, D.C.: The Heritage Foundation, 1980), pp. 13-29.

[16] Kent de Van Liere and Riley E. Dunlap, "The Social Basis of Environmental Concern: A Review of Hypotheses, Explanations, and Empirical Evidence," *Public Opinion Quarterly* (1980), p. 194.

whimsical argument that the wealthy should be allowed to reap this reward for having to confront high marginal tax rates.

The transfer of wealth from the relatively poor citizen to the relatively wealthy or highly educated wilderness user has two components. First is the opportunity cost discussed above and second is the cost of managing the system. Given that the 1964 Act requires passive management, this cost is fairly low; yet, it is not borne by wilderness users. Publicly supported wilderness lands are similar to publicly supported operas: while in principle available to all, they are used primarily by the relatively wealthy and well-educated. While such outcomes may be justified, they are usually neglected or ignored by wilderness advocates.

Privatization and Farsightedness

Many political decisions suggest that the relevant discount rate for politicians seeking reelection approaches infinity beyond two, four, or six years. While the speculator has the opportunity to capture benefits far in the future, the politician is constrained by elections, and he must weigh the expected evaluation of the mean voter.[17] Harold Demsetz, first of a growing number of economists who understands this problem, notes that "communal property means that future generations must speak for themselves. No one has yet estimated the costs of such a conservation."[18]

Most economists seem to believe that a market setting leads to robbing natural resources from future generations. In a particularly clear statement, a highly regarded resource economist writes:

> Generally, markets are considered fair only if all those affected by the outcomes are present in the market (without externalities) and the distribution of market power is considered fair. In the case of deciding which new (energy) supplies to develop, the distribution of market power is indeed uneven: the present generation controls the total stock of resources, leaving future generations with no voice in today's decisions.[19]

Another respected source of such wisdom is found in Robert Solow's 1973 Ely Lecture: "We know in general that even well-functioning markets may fail to allocate resources properly over time. The reason, I have suggested, is because, in the nature of the case, the future brings no en-

---

[17] For a discussion, see John Baden and Richard L. Stroup, "Transgenerational Equity and Natural Resources: Or, Too Bad We Don't Have Coal Rangers," in *Bureaucracy vs. Environment*, pp. 203-216.

[18] Demsetz, "Toward a Theory of Property Rights."

[19] J. V. Krutilla and R. T. Page, "Paying Tomorrow for Energy Today," *Resources* (June 1975).

dowment of its own to whatever market actually exists."[20] An even stronger case is suggested in the following: "In the extreme case, future generations cannot compensate the present for forgoing the mildest satisfactions; even the very survival of mankind is at stake."[21]

Except for Demsetz's insight, these sentiments may depress those who see economics as a way to increase understanding of policy issues. The literature often disseminates error and confusion. We certainly expect a market system based on privately held rights to yield different results than those produced by a system where decisions on resources are made collectively. In deciding whether a resource should be exploited now or later, the decision maker compares *current* with expected value in the highest future use discounted to the present. When current exploitation promises greater net benefits than preservation, the decision maker is expected to choose current exploitation rather than preservation. The problem, of course, is in the estimation of factors that are uncertain and often subjective. For any specified population and resource, people are likely to have widely differing opinions on when the resource should be developed or, more specifically, whether current exploitation is best.

In a democratic contest where politicians respond to the preferences of the average voter, the relevant question is whether the majority believes that the resources should be exploited now. The righthand tail of the distribution, composed of those who think it more valuable to preserve the resource for the future, will be outvoted. In a simple market situation involving the same individuals and the same resource, those who are most optimistic about high future values will control the decision process. The highest bid will prevail, and the highest bidders will be those who believe the resource will be worth more in the future. Thus, the tendency is for those with the *strongest* preservation values to control.

If a serious "resource crunch" occurs, only the most naive or optimistic would want to entrust wilderness areas to the whims and fluctuations of the political system. Some lost their political virginity in disputes over the building of the Alaskan pipeline, and many remember the conflict with dismay. Should a similar perturbation of supply occur, those who place a high value on wilderness would be ahead if they entrusted its preservation to private hands.

Examination of the windfall profits tax on oil illustrates an additional problem. The political response to the politically induced shortage of oil produced mostly negative outcomes that are likely to burden us for

---

[20] Robert Solow, "The Economics of Resources or the Resources of Economics," *American Economic Review* 64 (May 1970).

[21] V. D. Lippit and K. Hamad, "Efficiency and Equity in Energy Generational Distribution," in *Sustainable Society*, ed. Dennis S. Pirages (New York: Praeger, 1977), pp. 285-299.

generations. One of those outcomes has been neglected by analysts, and it augers ill for the preservation of wilderness systems.

When the windfall profits tax was imposed, a clear and unavoidable message was issued: if investors are prudent and farsighted enough to hold resources off the market until their value increases, the benefits flowing from conservation will be expropriated via taxes. Thus, the incentive to conserve materially and substantially is reduced. While it would be easy to hold stocks of strategic minerals privately until an emergency arose, the government convincingly has told us that the investor will not be able to capture the benefits of his prudence. Within this distorted system, we cannot expect the private sector to hold an adequate buffer stock of strategic minerals. The second order implications of the windfall profit tax include an increased probability that wilderness areas will be desecrated in an accelerated search for strategic minerals if our foreign sources are cut off. In the absence of private buffer stocks, minerals in wilderness areas may be the only source available in the medium run.

Fortunately, there is an alternative. In the interest of preserving wilderness land, a negative tax could be imposed on speculative profits.[22] Even though "speculator" has become a derisive term, aside from exaggerated cases of monopoly, the criticism of speculators conflicts with the announced preferences of environmentalists and conservationists. Individuals who favor deferred consumption advocate saving resources for the future. This is exactly the function of the speculator, who outbids those who prefer to consume now so he can conserve for his future profit. Although current consumers may object to speculators for driving up the market price and reducing consumption, those in the future should be grateful if the speculator guesses correctly. The key point is that successful speculators benefit future consumers at the expense of those in the present. With this point in mind, we can see why those who advocate wilderness preservation areas should advocate stockpiling strategic minerals. Stockpiling surely would be encouraged by the imposition of a negative tax on speculative profits.

Privatization and Economizing on Good Will and Understanding

A social order based on clear, enforceable property rights and the rule of willing consent strongly encourages cooperation and agreement. As Ludwig von Mises states in *Human Action*:

The social philosophy of paternal despotism laid stress upon the divine mission of kings and autocrats predestined to rule the peoples. The

---

[22] Richard L. Stroup and John Baden, "Conversations with the Beyond: A Negative Tax on Speculative Profits," *Taxing & Spending* 3 (Summer 1980), p. 67.

[classical] liberal retorted that the operation of an unhampered market, in which the consumer—i.e., every citizen—is sovereign, brings about more satisfactory results than the decrees of anointed rulers. Observe the functioning of the market system, they said, and you will discover in it too the finger of God.[23]

Moving beyond the classical liberal, von Mises goes on to state:

> A pre-eminent common interest, the preservation and further intensification of social cooperation, becomes paramount and obliterates all essential collisions. Catallactic (exchange) competition is substituted for biological competition. It makes for harmony of the interests of all members of society....

> This is the meaning of the theorem of the harmony of the rightly understood interests of all members of the market society. When the classical economists made this statement, they were trying to stress two points: first, that everybody is interested in the preservation of the social division of labor, the system that multiplies the productivity of human efforts. Second, that in the market society consumers' demands ultimately directs all productive activities.[24]

While von Mises is unlikely to sway the skeptic, his logic may. Given that scarcity is an elemental fact of human existence, not everyone can be satisfied. In some institutional forms, such as the game of poker, the net result is zero sum; one party's gain must be balanced by another's loss. When resources are allocated by the political system, the relevant currency is political power. Since most voters are rationally ignorant about the details and implications of public policy, extremist positions are needed to gain attention, and conflict can be expected. Political decision making, however, is commonly negative sum, and the contrast with market decisions based on the rule of willing consent is extreme. People do not consent willingly to decisions when they expect to be made worse off because of them. In the political system, citizens are coerced to pay for such environmental atrocities as the Teton Dam, terracing the Bitterroot National Forest, resource planning that costs more than the resource is worth, deficit timber sales, and a litany of other violations of environmental sensitivity and economic efficiency.

One might infer from the above that enemies should be chosen at least as carefully as friends in the political system. We can easily see why James Watt might be considered the National Honorary Membership and Contributions Chairman for the environmental movement. Although most of the mainline environmental groups have called for Watt's resignation—including the Sierra Club, the National Audubon Society, the

---

[23] Ludwig von Mises, *Human Action*, rev. ed. (Chicago: Contemporary Books, 1966), p. 239. Originally published in 1949 by Yale University Press.
[24] *Ibid.*, pp. 673-674.

National Wildlife Federation, Friends of the Earth, the Isaac Walton League, and the Wilderness Society—the officers of these groups recognize Watt's contribution to their membership and financial programs. They reason that visible enemies, especially those who enjoy Presidential Cabinet status, are more valuable than the best of friends. The threat or the realization of environmental atrocities does far more for the welfare of the bureaucrats who direct environmental organizations than does calm, quiet, and successful resource management.

The June 1982 issue of the Wyoming Heritage Society *Newsletter* gives us a better understanding of the situation:

> [Environmental] organizations have expanded their membership tremendously by riding on Jim Watt's back...[They] are distorting the truth and especially inflame the emotions of those who live far from Wyoming. The response is more contributions to the ever-growing war chest that is being used to obstruct energy development and even the leasing of grazing lands. Their purpose is to add more than two million acres to Wyoming wilderness and to postpone any short or long-term non-wilderness designations of public lands....It's pretty hard to get the average American excited over the need for an additional oil well, a new mine, or dependable and reliable grazing policies for agriculture. It's much easier to say that America's west will be destroyed by resource development unless the American people support the environmentalists and those Americans who believe the propaganda are pouring millions into national environmental organizations.[25]

The *Newsletter* also contains quotes from executives of two leading environmental organizations. Michael McCloskey, Executive Director of the Sierra Club, states:

> At this very moment the Sierra Club is at work around the clock to support our dramatic petition drives with intensive political action,...Unless you and I act immediately, we will surely witness the destroying of lands needed for our national parks, the dispoiling [sic] of pristine wilderness areas, and the irreparable damage to our air and water....[26]

William A. Turnage of the Wilderness Society reportedly writes:

> I am writing to warn you that if James Watt, the Secretary of the Interior, has his way, America will have fewer clear-running trout streams, fewer game-filled forests for you and me to enjoy...James Watt wants to establish energy and mineral development as the dominant use of all public lands, even including wilderness...but...Secretary Watt can succeed only if he, and his hand-maidens in industry, convince the public that America's resources are locked up.[27]

---

[25] Wyoming Heritage Society, *Newsletter*, June 1982, p. 1.
[26] *Ibid.*, p. 3.
[27] *Ibid.*

McCloskey and Turnage are not unkind individuals, but the institutional structure surrounding them rewards this kind of behavior. Unfortunately, they have no monopoly on bad manners. In such an environment, industry gains support by referring to the privileged elites who lock up the nation's resources, depriving honest, hardworking men and women of jobs so the privileged can recreate in their private wilderness playgrounds. William Dresher, former Dean of the University of Arizona's School of Mines, discusses wilderness in the following terms:

> The highest form of land dedication, indeed! In other words, our public lands are being treated like the sacred cows of India—not to be touched or molested, regardless of our need. Obviously, this is the intent of our government, as time after time it places impediments in the way of domestic mining industry.[28]

Such statements indicated the militant and even strident tones frequently used by commentators on both sides of the wilderness issue. Because Congress and the executive branch have discretionary control over wilderness and can change the rules of the game, they are under constant pressure to change land use and patterns. There will always be groups seeking "rents"; that is, they want to use the land without paying full opportunity cost. This transfer activity is pervasive in our society and is especially obvious in the management of wilderness.

Asking whether a 100,000- or 1,000,000-acre wilderness area should be preserved or used to produce oil, gas, and minerals is asking the wrong question. In those few areas where the values seriously compete, it is possible and probably desirable that the values from both outputs be sought. The appropriate question is: How can we get the best combination of wilderness, mineral, and other values out of this particular piece of land? To the public land manager who must invite comments but not bids from all comers, the problems are severe. The list of competitive users may be endless for a particular area, and it is sadistic to require public managers to make these decisions without the benefit of price data.

Privatization and a Harmony of Interests

The National Audubon Society is concerned with environmental quality in general and wildlife habitat in particular.[29] In addition to a substantial educational and publishing operation, the Society also owns 75 wildlife sanctuaries.[30] The Paul J. Rainey Wildlife Sanctuary in Ver-

---

[28] William Dresher, *Raw Materials for Industry: Our Next Major Crisis*, undated pamphlet, p. 10.

[29] For more on this, see John Baden and Richard Stroup, "Saving the Wilderness: A Radical Proposal," *Reason* 13 (July 1981), pp. 28–36.

[30] There are also approximately 100 refuges operated by local chapters of the Audubon Society. See *Islands of Life: The National Audubon Society Sanctuaries* (New York: National Audubon Society, n.d.); and "1981 Fact Sheet" (pamphlet distributed by the National Audubon Society, New York, 1981).

milion Parish, Louisiana, is a 26,000-acre bird refuge that is so sensitive that tourists are unwelcome. Even unmonitored bird watchers are forbidden entry. The refuge is controlled and managed for otter, mink, deer, reptiles, hundreds of thousands of birds—and oil and natural gas wells.

Because the Rainey Preserve is in private hands, there is every incentive to use the resources efficiently. The timing, placement, operation, and structure of their oil operation on the sanctuary is programmed carefully with the seasonal habitat requirements of the wildlife residents. In the Audubon Society's description of the Rainey Sanctuary, they make the following statement: "There are oil wells in Rainey which are potential sources of pollution. Yet Audubon's experience during the past few decades indicated that oil can be extracted without measurable damage to the marsh. Extra precautions to prevent pollution have proven effective."[31]

Revenue derived from the wells is used to buy additional preserves and achieve Audubon Society goals. This is clearly a positive sum game where all participants win: the birds and wildlife have their habitat preserved, the public gets its oil, and Audubon receives revenues to purchase additional preserves. The outcome is a function of property rights that lead to cooperative and efficient behavior.

Contrast Audubon's actions on their own lands with their pronouncements against exploration on the public lands. The difference in harmony between political and market decision making is extreme. In a recent "Emergency Dispatch" to Audubon Society members, for example, President Russell Peterson states: "The National Audubon Society is entering a battle. A battle we must win. If we lose, we will witness the irrevocable destruction of much of America's natural heritage."[32] Another memo complains: "Secretary [of Interior] Watt has undertaken a program involving land exchanges and transfers to the detriment of federal holdings, and has supported the divestiture to transfer of federal responsibility over the nation's public lands—a program which will ultimately lead to over-exploitation by indiscriminate private interests."[33]

To assure environmentally and economically sound land use policies, wilderness lands could be transferred in fee simple terms to environmental groups. Although such an action would generate a tremendous windfall gain to groups not noted for their disadvantaged status, it might be a tolerable price to pay for the generated benefits. It is important to

---

[31] *Islands of Life.*, p. 19.

[32] Russell W. Peterson, "Emergency Dispatch," (memo addressed to National Audubon Society members, n.d.).

[33] Memo to Russell W. Peterson from Bill Butler, distributed to National Audubon Society members, n.d., p. 2. See also National Audubon Society, "1981 Annual Report"; *idem*, "A Double Bill: Coming Soon to Your Public Lands" (pamphlet distributed to Audubon Society members, n.d.); and Russell W. Peterson, "No Mandate to Destroy Environmental Laws," *Bozeman Daily Chronicle* (Montana), August 13, 1981, p. 4.

remember that the incentives faced by the professional managers of these organizations as rent seekers in the grants economy, if not full owners and residual claimants, are dramatically different than those faced by the same individuals as political adversaries.[34]

The mining of strategic minerals must be concentrated if it is to pay. Less than one million acres have been mined for nonfuel minerals in the last fifty years in the United States, and 90 percent of the free world's mineral requirements are supplied by less than 1,200 mines.[35] A small area of wilderness land used for mineral production might make a tremendous difference in terms of America's mineral independence. Clearly it is inefficient to lock up such areas when a relatively insignificant portion of that land could yield huge mineral wealth and possibly strengthen national security. When it is reported that the federal government has withdrawn two-thirds of the nation's land from mining entry,[36] politically active representatives become increasingly agitated.[37]

Large mineral deposits probably would not be located in areas of critical, environmental concern. Lands with high economic but low ecological value should be made available for development. Conversely, those with high ecological but low economic value should be left alone in a market setting. Areas with both ecological and economic importance should be managed by groups with the expertise to weigh the potential damage to the environment against the potential profits. The obvious way to accomplish this is to make environmental groups the owners of the holdings; they would be residual claimants able to garner any benefits they generate through added resource values. Under these conditions, the new owners' groups likely would emulate the Audubon Society's actions on the Rainey Sanctuary.

If wilderness and restricted land were transferred in fee simple terms to an environmental interest group, the organization would have the opportunity to lease the mineral rights and obtain the royalties. How would the organization behave? Given that the managers and directors of the interest group are intelligent and dedicated, they will attempt, in accord with their values, to maximize the potential value of the resource. Assuming that they have a general interest in wilderness values

[34] There is such a variety of distribution plans that might be used under such a system that the subject cannot be properly addressed in this paper, but see John Baden, "Diversity, Stability, and Adaptability in Economic and Ecological Systems" (paper presented at a conference on Politics vs. Policy: The Public Land Dilemma, Utah State University, Logan, April 21–23, 1982).

[35] Report by the Comptroller General to the Congress of the United States, *The U.S. Mining and Mineral-Processing Industry: An Analysis of Trends and Implications* (Washington, D.C.: Government Printing Office, 1979).

[36] Gary Bennethum and L. Courtland Lee, "Is Our Account Overdrawn?" *Mining Congress Journal* (September 1975), pp. 33–48.

[37] See House of Representatives, Committee on Armed Services, *Hearings on National Defense Stockpile*, 97th Congress, 1st session (Washington, D.C.: Government Printing Office, June 1981).

and are not oriented toward any specific land area, they will carefully evaluate the contribution that this land could make to their goals.

For example, if the area had a titanium deposit expected to yield a million dollars worth of net benefits, they would consider developing it. They would confront three basic questions: first, how much profit would such an activity yield? Second, how much additional wilderness land or services could be bought with that profit? Third, how can management of these lands permit mineral extraction while minimizing the impact on the wilderness features of the land; that is, how can the value of the joint products be maximized?

With fee simple title to the land, the wilderness group is forced by its own criteria to consider the opportunity costs of total nondevelopment. Rather than blindly opposing the extraction of commercially valuable resources from the land, they must focus on obtaining these resources while maintaining to an optimal degree the wilderness character of the area. Different incentives lead to different behavior.

This change in the rules of the federal mineral game could yield enormous benefits. With land in private hands, all interested parties would become more constructive in their thinking and in their language. Instead of discrediting the goals of others, they would be concerned with how desired ends could be best achieved at the least cost to others. The owners would think this way in order to capture more revenues, selling off the highest valued package of rights that is consistent with their own values. Similarly, a buyer of mining rights or of conservation easements wants to purchase his valued package at the least cost to the seller, and thus, to himself. In addition, the unlimited wants of every party are forced into priority classes. The *most important* land rights will be purchased and declarations that every contested acre is priceless become suitably absurd.

Even people in single-minded pursuit of profits or of narrow wilderness goals will act *as if* other social goals mattered. Indeed, they may *seek out* higher valued uses of their own acreage, using profits to obtain new means to satisfy their own narrow goals. After all, it is their actions, not the worthiness of their goals, that should concern the rest of society. While not all good things go together, some do; and the analytical leverage of political economy can be used to expand them. Given a scarcity of good will, we will be ahead if we design institutions that economize upon it. Private property is a key institution for economizing on our supply.

Implementation

Economic efficiency and environmental quality would be enhanced if public wilderness areas were transferred to environmental groups such as the Audubon Society, the Wilderness Society, or the Sierra Club.

The primary goal of this paper is to advance this idea and its underlying logic, not to specify proposals for implementing policy. Although the implementation process is important, the form it takes is less critical than ensuring that the transfers are made. Thus, the following is suggestive rather than definitive.

Any successful transfer mechanism would have to take into account the potentials for rent dissipation and the benefits from reducing transaction costs. Under a sufficiently perverse system, most of the benefits from privatization could be dissipated by the efforts of those competing for the property rights in the resource. A straight auction or lottery for each area would have significant advantages. The simplest methods should be considered first, since they are probably optimal for certain areas. Some reasonable alternatives to bidding and lottery systems are presented below.

Coase's 1960 article, "The Problem of Social Costs," shows that efficiency is fostered if initial allocations of property rights are identical to those that would develop through the process of voluntary exchange. If the resource is allocated initially to those who value it most, the transaction costs that accompany exchanges can be eliminated.

Groups are eligible for exchange only if they existed prior to the introduction of the legislation mandating the land transfers. This constraint is necessary to preclude groups being created for the sole purpose of capturing the newly available resources. Huge bureaucratic rents obviously will be available to the recipients of those wilderness lands that contain concentrations of minerals or energy sources, and many would be tempted to subvert the process to get a piece of that pie. Politicians and specialists in the policy arena undoubtedly would be extraordinarily creative in designing alternative implementation plans. Thus, the two proposals outlined below provide only a first cut at the problem.

The first alternative involves identifying those wilderness areas that are appropriate for transfer. These areas would be nominated by the eligible environment groups and would not exceed 1/20th of the total wilderness area in 1982. Presumably, these groups would first nominate sensitive or threatened areas. A joint congressional committee would then select those areas that would be transferred to private ownership.

In exchange or as payment for the land, each organization would agree to provide certain services. For example, organization A might develop and maintain five public campgrounds, forty miles of hiking trails, a nature center, accredited nature study programs for high school and college students, and a return to the federal treasury of 40 percent of any mineral or energy lease revenues that might be obtained from development. Organization B might enter a competing "bid" with an alternative menu of opportunities. Each bid would include an agreement to provide easements guaranteeing public access and covenants restricting certain activities, such as nuclear disposal sites or other actions presumed to be incompatible with a sensitive environment. Provisions for monitoring performance also must be included in the contracts. Even though the leaders of nonprofit environmental groups will not be residual claimants, they can capture the substantial rents that flow from sound resource management. This provides strong incentives for acting in an efficient and responsible manner.

The second form of bidding (which could be mixed with the first) would involve a different *quid pro quo*. The nominating process would be identical, but after the areas were nominated and selected, each organization would contract to provide an environmental service in exchange for the land it desired. For example, organization C might propose to reclaim, revegetate, and improve stripmined and previously unreclaimed areas. Organization D might propose to reforest areas recently destroyed by fire or assume managerial responsibility for wild horses and burros in a certain area.

The second method of transfer has certain advantages over the first. Given that membership in environmental groups is marked by a bimodal distribution of income, this second option would enable them to utilize their members, especially college students, whose opportunity costs of time are often quite low. These organizations could co-sponsor programs with universities, such as the Land Reclamation Program at Montana State University, combining fieldwork with coursework. For relatively low wages, student members could complete the tasks contracted for by the organization while obtaining university credit.

In policy analysis, there are no perfect, cost-free solutions. While privatization has ecological, economic, and equity advantages over continued public ownership of wilderness lands, such a change must occur in a political environment in which people are predominantly self-interested and rationally ignorant of most policies and programs. Only by organizing special interest groups will it be possible to successfully execute such programs. Given prevailing sentiments, it is unlikely that these groups will respond to the opportunities described above until they perceive both a fundamental threat to the areas they cherish and an opportunity to improve their organization's position. I cannot, of course, predict when we may be subjected to an energy or strategic minerals cutoff, but both are real possibilities. Should they occur, the privatization of our wilderness lands may be our reward for surviving the struggle.

8

The Case for Privatizing Government Owned Timberlands

by Barney Dowdle

Introduction

The purpose of the present paper is to argue the case for privatizing commercial timberlands that are owned and managed by government: federal, state, or local. The principal use of these lands is commercial timber production, an activity that is best conducted by the private sector.

Evidence is accumulating increasingly that government has been a failure in the business of timber production. It is economically inefficient and costly to taxpayers, it perpetuates inequities, and the environmental benefits that are allegedly produced have been greatly overstated.

The provision of nonpriced "multiple-use" benefits, such as recreation, wildlife habitats, visual amenities, and watershed protection is not a sufficient argument for the continued production of timber by government, as many will suggest. Private timberlands also produce multiple-use benefits, and they do so more efficiently than government.

Timbered states that have very little government ownership, such as Maine, Vermont, and Georgia, enjoy multiple-use benefits similar to those of such states as Washington, Oregon, and California, where over half the commercial timberland is in government ownership. The present argument for privatization, it should be emphasized, does not pertain to national or state parks, wilderness areas, or to other exclusive-use areas where commercial timber production is not permitted.

Removing government from the business of timber production would eliminate some fundamental incompatibilities from our economic system, and free enterprise would be permitted to function in important areas of the economy from which it is now excluded. Some local and regional economics, which are based on wood-processing industries, are now almost completely dependent upon government timber supplies. The interface between private timber production and wood processing (free enterprise) and government timber production (state ownership and centralized planning, that is, socialism) is an inherently untenable and unstable situation.

For very good reasons, the American people are reluctant to permit the U.S. economy to become significantly dependent upon socialist economies for raw materials. This is, however, effectively what has been done to the domestic wood-processing industry in several parts of the West.

The consequences of this situation are likely much worse than is generally understood. Government timber production is highly politicized and bureaucraticized. The general public hears mostly the inflated claims of interest groups and the self-serving statements of government bureaucracies. Disinterested analyses and accurate accountability are difficult to obtain.

Privatization of government timberlands (denationalization) is the best means of correcting a failed experiment in socialism. Economic disruptions, which are currently occurring in the timber, wood-processing, and dependent industries, would be alleviated; coexistence problems between the public and private sectors would be eliminated; counterproductive government regulations could be abandoned; and taxpayers' burdens would be lightened.

The environmental impact of privatization would be minimal, and could be positive. Inefficient and wasteful government timber production is commonly associated with unwarranted environmental disruption. Too much land is used to produce too little timber. The most obvious examples are excessive road construction and unnecessarily wide dispersal of logging activities across government timberlands.

Background Statistics

About 27 percent of the nation's total acreage of commercial timberlands is owned by federal, state, and local governments. This includes about 90 million acres of the national forests, which are managed by the Forest Service, U.S. Department of Agriculture; 10 million acres managed by the Bureau of Land Management (BLM); and about 30 million acres managed by various state and local governments. Most government timberlands are located in the West. This is a result of the settlement of the U.S. from east to west, and the fact that the decision to put government in the timber production business was made around 1900. At that time, most remaining public domain timberlands were located in the West.

Because of the concentration of past timber harvests in the private sector, 63 percent of the total softwood sawtimber inventory is currently in government ownership. The Forest Service alone controls 51 percent of the total softwood sawtimber inventory. For the first 50 years of its existence (1905-1955) the Forest Service contributed only 3 percent to total softwood sawtimber output. Softwood sawtimber is the raw materials base for the production of lumber and plywood. Both products are important components of the housing industry.

The reason private timberlands were harvested first is that they were generally located at lower elevations, closer to wood-processing facilities. Private timber was, therefore, more economical to harvest. Politically inspired statements that the private sector has depleted its own timber and now wants to do the same with public timber ignore the fact that this historical sequence of timber harvesting was economically efficient. A corollary is that there was not much demand for public timber in the past; now that there is, it would be timely to take advantage of opportunities being presented.

Myths of Government Timber Production

A useful point of departure in arguing the case for privatization of government timberlands is to address the question: Why is government in the business of producing timber in the U.S.? Government doesn't produce corn or wheat. Why should it produce timber?

The quick answer to this question is that it should not. The case for government timber production is based largely on myth. The federal government became involved in the business largely as a result of historical accident, and state and local governments followed the federal precedent.

This historical accident was a consequence of two fundamental errors: (1) a misinterpretation of the migratory practices of the lumber industry during the settlement stages of U.S. growth and development, and (2) unsound forestry theory regarding the economics of timber production.

The fact that the lumber industry was migratory during the 19th and early 20th centuries was widely interpreted as evidence of market failure. As is well-known, during this period the U.S. was attempting to build an economic system based on private property and decentralized markets. Such a system is generally labelled as "free enterprise," "capitalism," or a "market economy," terms that are used interchangeably here. Government is understood to be responsible for certain activities in an economic system of this kind. In general, however, its role in production is minimal.

The goal of constructing a free enterprise economic system has origins in the visions and plans of the Founding Fathers. Such an economic system, they believed, would maximize individual freedom and productive efficiency. Building this system necessitated that lands acquired by the federal government be alienated into private ownership.

The massive scale on which land transfers took place created considerable confusion and misunderstanding. Fraud and theft were common, although the values involved were much less than is commonly suggested. Most important, costs of building a free enterprise economic system in some areas of production, including timber, were misinterpreted as evidence that the system did not work.

When timberlands were acquired by private interests, not uncommonly the timber was harvested, and cut-over lands were then abandoned. The market system, it appeared, would harvest existing stands of mature timber, but it would not grow new timber crops. Bad forestry theory, which is discussed below, lent further support to this incorrect conclusion.

Since wood products were important to the nation's economic well-being, and forests provided important secondary benefits such as watershed protection and wildlife habitat, an understandable conclusion was that public domain forest lands should be retained in government ownership; timber production would be a nationalized industry. Public land disposal policies were changed to accommodate this conclusion, and government was in the business of producing timber.

A Bureau of Forestry was established in 1901 to manage the newly acquired nationalized timberlands, and forestry schools quickly came into existence to produce professional foresters to staff it. As would be expected, forestry students were taught that the market system (laissez faire, as they called it) didn't work; under their guidance, timber production would be based on "scientific planning." This legacy is still reflected in forest management curricula, and distrust of the market system is widespread within the forestry profession. The Bureau of Forestry became the Forest Service in 1905.

What is a correct interpretation of the migratory practices of the lumber industry historically? Simply stated, the market was reducing an overabundance of naturally endowed timber inventories. It was behaving as expected, given the conditions that existed at the time.

In a market economy, timber will not be grown if it is cheaper to buy. Plentiful supplies of virgin timber were available in the U. S. until the early 1950s, and timber prices remained low until that time. Second growth timber crops, which would have provided a raw materials base for a permanently located lumber industry, could not be produced economically on cut-over timberlands because of low timber prices.

Predictably, the center of gravity of lumber production shifted toward low-priced virgin timber. Lumbermen would not have survived had they attempted to comply with the admonishments of foresters and conservationists to grow timber on cut-over lands in order to maintain stable operations and dependent communities.

The social costs of a migratory lumber industry were undeniably high, but this experience is not unique in U. S. history. Agriculture, mining, railroads, and textiles also left high social costs in their wakes as they were transformed by economic growth. The lumber industry is unique, however, because its migratory practices led to the nationalization of an important basic industry.

The forestry myth that the market system doesn't work in timber production because of a long growth period was obviously reinforced by the migratory practices of the lumber industry. The substance of this myth, which has enjoyed a lengthy history in the evolution of forest management theory, is that private investors have no incentive to plant and grow timber because the maturation period of their investments is likely to exceed their life expectancy. Apart from altruism, who is willing to bear the cost of planting a tree if he doesn't expect to be alive to realize the gains from its harvest?

The answer to this question, which also dispels the myth, is that anyone should be willing to plant a tree who can reasonably assume to get a return on his investment. Moreover, he doesn't have to wait until the tree reaches maturity and is harvested. If markets exist for goods-in-process, so that old men can sell their assets to young men, then the market system and profit seeking will ensure that timber is grown. The development of private tree farming in the U. S. provides ample and convincing evidence to support this conclusion. Trees are often planted, and immature timber stands subsequently sold.

The "Allowable Cut" Concept

The establishment of a system of government timber production, based on the belief that this was an area of market failure, led to the rejection of economics as a relevant guide to timber management. An "annual allowable cut" concept (AAC), which is devoid of economic considerations, was adopted by government agencies to determine timber outputs. The purpose of constraining timber outputs to levels determined by AAC calculations was to produce an "even flow" of timber over time.

Even flow would supposedly ensure industry and community "stability;" the social costs of a migratory lumber industry would, therefore, be eliminated. That even flow would create a timber supply rigidity and disrupt timber markets does not appear to have been considered by its early proponents. Government foresters are still reluctant to debate this possibility in spite of overwhelming evidence that it is occurring.

The AAC and even flow concepts were introduced into the U. S. from western Europe where they had evolved in the management of forests which were subject to common use. As is well-known, resources used in common are susceptible to overexploitation unless use is regulated. Fish and wildlife populations, which are managed as common property or "fugitive" resources, are subject to bag limits to prevent their depletion. AACs for timber are essentially bag limits on trees. Likewise, their adoption in the U. S. was to prevent profit seeking from depleting timber stands and, thereby, causing a timber "famine."

A property rights explanation of collectivized timber production in the U. S. is that early American foresters and conservationists did not distinguish correctly between: (1) the possibility of depletion which is inherent in the exploitation of a common property resource, and (2) the expectation of continued production of timber on privately owned lands following the initial depletion of excess timber inventories. The market system cannot work in the first case, because there is no market. In the second case, production will be undertaken after the inventory correction has been made and timber prices have risen.

The existence of this logical error is evident in the analogies that conservationists have often made between buffalo herds and beaver populations, which were exploited as fugitive resources, and timber, which, apart from theft, was not. This logical error is understandable. The visible evidence indicated that stocks of all three resources were being depleted.

That the price system would function to prevent the depletion of timber, but that its nonexistence precluded its saving buffalo and beaver, was undoubtedly a subtlety of economic reasoning, which had little chance of guiding policy in the reform atmosphere that characterized American politics near the turn of the century.

The Forest Service and the BLM have gone beyond traditional concepts of AAC and even flow in planning the management of commercial timber inventories under their jurisdictions and have adopted a concept known as "non-declining even flow." The latter variant of even flow precludes reductions in an initially determined AAC. Non-declining even flow has been highly controversial because inventories of physically over-mature timber cannot be harvested at economically justifiable rates. Over-mature timber, as in the case of other crops, is subject to the infirmities of old age. Unless harvested, it will eventually die and decay.

Disruptive Effects of Government Timber Production

In addition to preventing economically desirable adjustments in inventories of over-mature timber, the even flow constraint prevents adjusting the quantities of timber sold to changes in demand. Timber prices are, therefore, highly volatile in markets which are impacted by government timber. The fact that government timber sales are not price responsive has contributed importantly to the present economic plight of the timber industry in the West, where government timber dominates the markets.

An even flow of timber forces buyers to speculate, to get timber un-

76

der contract at bid prices that reflect what future prices are expected to be. Speculation is encouraged because down payments on government timber contracts are minimal. Payments are made as timber is harvested.

Fueled by the inflationary expectations of the late 1970s, speculation for government timber was rampant, and bid prices escalated to unprecedented highs. Rising interest rates and the collapse in the housing industry burst this speculative bubble. Expectedly, those who were caught have since been seeking government relief. The State of Washington has adopted legislation that would terminate some contracts for state owned timber. This legislation, however, will be tested in the courts.

At the federal level, the timber industry, represented mostly by affected Westerners, has been lobbying for legislation to provide some form of contract relief. Whether or not relief will be obtained, and by how much, remains to be seen. Opposition to this legislation is based on the argument that relief would be an unwarranted bailout; speculators should have been more prudent, and a bailout would set a bad precedent. In addition, relief benefits would be distributed disproportionately across timber-producing regions, hence regional timber markets would be disrupted. The South, which has very little government timber, would be most disadvantaged. This is reflected in opposition from that region to relief legislation.

Regional timber inventory and production statistics suggest the potential magnitude of interregional market disruptions. The Pacific Northwest (western Oregon and western Washington) has a softwood sawtimber inventory that the Forest Service has recently estimated to be 544 billion board feet. Sixty-nine percent of this inventory is owned and managed by government agencies. Nearly 10 billion board feet of government timber is reportedly under contract at prices that preclude harvesting without causing substantial losses to buyers.

The softwood sawtimber inventory in the South is reported to be 340 billion board feet, only 14 percent of which is owned and managed by government agencies. At present, the annual timber harvest in the South is 22 percent greater than in the Pacific Northwest, a difference largely indicative of the economic inefficiencies of government timber production.

The controversy over contract relief merely emphasizes the shortcomings of government timber production. Bad government policies have disrupted timber markets, and have led to more bad policies adopted in attempts to correct the initial disruptions. Not uncommonly, the problems are thereby aggravated. The owners of government timber, the taxpayers, bear most of the costs of these exercises in economic folly. That these costs are evidence of a failed experiment in socialism has yet to catch the public's attention.

Multiple-Use Management

Multiple-use management is commonly cited as justification for government ownership of timberlands. Is this a valid argument? Or is it primarily bureaucratic public relations? This question is difficult to answer, but public relations seem to dominate multiple-use arguments; there is little evidence to substantiate many government agency claims.

The multiple-use concept of government timber management results in significant economic inefficiencies because of the arbitrary manner in which the mix of timber and other multiple-use outputs is determined. Formal economic criteria and relative price information are not used for the purpose of determining what the overall output mix will be. A major reason for this practice is that multiple-use outputs, such as recreation, visual amenities, wildlife refuges, and related benefits, are provided to consumers at a zero price.

Tradeoffs between the production of timber, which has a price, and other multiple-use benefits, which do not, are made largely on the basis of *ad hoc* administrative allowances. These allowances originate in the opinions of agency experts and external political pressures. "Public involvement" programs have institutionalized the latter part of this process. As might be expected, political pressures tend to be seriously misleading in terms of evaluating the performance of the system.

Individuals and oranized groups have a tendency to use emotion and misinformation and to exaggerate their preferences in their efforts to push for the management alternatives that are most to their liking. In attempting to cater to such political pressures, government agencies have incurred substantial increases in management costs. The costs of harvesting and preparing timber for sale have risen enormously. Likewise, timber values (economic rents) have been dissipated because of the constraints imposed on timber management and harvesting activities.

Once the test of prices, costs, and profits, or a benefit-cost variant thereof, is discarded as a guide to management decisions and as a measure of accountability, other means of performing these functions become largely meaningless. This has occurred in multiple-use management. Government agencies are apt to issue gratuitous statements that existing management is in the public interest. Questions of who benefits and who pays, and how much, become very difficult to answer.

In many cases, the alleged benefits of multiple-use management are, at best, dubious, and at worst, nonexistent. Timber that is left standing to provide roadside visual amenities or to protect streams is commonly blown down by high winds, only to be removed later in costly salvage operations. Logging debris is piled at great expense, such that it can be burned under cloud cover to prevent smoke visibility. "View sheds" are established, which require that large portions of an area contain timber

78

of no less than an arbitrarily specified age. Harvest age is thereby increased along with capital carrying charges.

The difficulty of estimating multiple-use benefits should not keep government agencies from reporting their production costs. If these costs were estimated objectively and made known, the general public would be better able to judge whether or not it is getting the kind of management that it wants. At present, these judgments are virtually impossible to make, and a credulous general public must accept the reports of its government timber managers that they are doing a good job. Considerable evidence exists that suggests this is not a stable situation, which could be an important factor leading to increased demands for privatization.

How Efficient Is Government Forestry?

The poor state of accountability for government timber production makes it difficult to determine the true state of government management. The importance of "externalities" in timber production further complicates this problem, but some crude estimates can be developed.

The Forest Service, for example, currently runs a cash flow deficit of approximately one billion dollars a year. This deficit is expected to increase. Meaningful accountability would require that capital costs be added to this cash flow deficit to determine the total cost of Forest Service management. Most Americans are painfully aware that the interest rate is not zero. Few understand, however, that the Forest Service manages billions of dollars worth of asset values for them as if interest rates were in fact zero.

Land and timber resources in the national forests that are classified as commercial include about 90 million acres of land—slightly more than a trillion board feet of softwood sawtimber inventory, more than half the nation's total. If commercial forest land were priced at $50 per acre, and timber at $100 per thousand board feet (both estimates are reasonably conservative), then the estimated value of the commercial land and timber resources on the national forests would be $104.5 billion. Support for this estimate has been provided by Marion Clawson who recently observed that "...the value of the lands and resources managed by the Forest Service and the BLM today approximates $500 billion—or half the national debt."

Assuming an interest rate of 10 percent, the capital costs of commercial land and timber resources on the national forests would be $10.4 billion per year. At present, these capital costs are not counted, nor are they reported. They are nevertheless legitimate costs against which benefits produced by the national forests must be weighed. If these capital costs are added to the billion dollars per year cash flow deficit that the

Forest Service incurs, then the annual cost of the national forests is about $11 billion per year greater than the revenues they produce.

Based on this estimate, the cost to the American people of maintaining the Forest Service in the business of timber production is nearly $50 per person per year. An interesting side note on this point is that it is illegal in most states for private corporations to assess stockholders their *pro rata* share of corporate deficits. Government agencies that produce timber make this assessment routinely. Private vice, it would seem, is a public virtue.

A further question which a calculation of this kind raises is whether or not society is receiving non-priced benefits commensurate with the costs that are being incurred. Perhaps so, but the absence of meaningful accountability effectively precludes the serious evaluation of this question. Since privately owned timberlands provide non-priced benefits too, it would be misleading to suggest that such benefits would disappear if the national forests were privatized.

Additionally, the present argument does not pertain to nearly 100 million acres of the national forests which are in wilderness and other exclusive use areas. Privatization of commercial timberlands on the national forests would not put the Forest Service out of business. It would merely remove it from the activities it handles inefficiently.

Suggestions for Privatization

In considering directions for the privatizing of commercial government timberlands, it should be noted that privatization of many of the resources on these lands is already taking place when timber, minerals, and other resources are sold. As they are sold, they are transferred to private ownership. The market then dictates their subsequent use. Land is the principal resource that is not sold. As noted above, the value of land is fractional in comparison with the value of commercial timber.

Privatization is, therefore, essentially a change in the timing and the rate at which government timber will be sold. Rather than metering timber into the market on the basis of annual allowable cut (AAC) calculations and the even flow concept, the entire inventory would be sold. The market system would then determine annual timber supplies.

It is not suggested here that government timber should be dumped on the market merely to get it privatized. It should be sold in such a way that (taxpayer) owners get a fair return. This could be done by selling government timber subject to a wide range of contractual arrangements. And by encouraging the development of a futures market in sales contracts, greater stability could be brought to timber markets. The counterproductive speculative tendencies that go along with existing institutional arrangements could be eliminated.

It would also be appropriate to drop the ban on log exports and to encourage foreign interests to make large, long-term purchases. This would increase demand and help to maximize returns. It is well-known that the Japanese are highly interested in long-term timber supply security. Access to government timber in the U. S. would provide such assurance, and timber sales to the Japanese would improve the U. S. balance of trade with that country.

Unless there were good reasons for selling land and timber together, they could be sold separately. If land is valuable as recreational property, then timber cover could be important. If land is sold separately, then it would be appropriate to sell it in units that would exploit economies of scale in growing future timber crops. Some land sales might also be made that would permit existing private landowners to develop more economical timber management units.

If land and timber in a given location are sold to different buyers, then the conditions of occupancy will affect the prices that each buyer is willing to pay. If the timber owner wanted to prolong his harvest date, then presumably he could rent land from the landowner for "warehousing" his timber. The market system is accustomed to handling such transactions.

Finally, a considerable amount of government timberland which is currently classified as commercial is likely to be submarginal for growing timber crops and other commercial uses. It is a well-known fact that much government timber production is heavily subsidized, either through appropriated funds or by cross-subsidizing from existing timber wealth. If submarginal lands are best used for some public purpose, such as wildlife refuges, watershed protection, or related activities, then it might be best to leave them in public jurisdiction.

A primary purpose of privatization, however, is to establish incentives that will result in the efficient use of resources. Government ownership and centrally planned management do not accomplish this objective. Private ownership and markets will.

The determination of what is commercial today depends upon existing technology and the relative prices of factor inputs and product outputs. These determinants of land values are subject to change over time. As long as land values reflect the present net worth of expected future uses, and property taxes are levied accordingly, then the fact that land may have negligible value today should not keep it from being privatized. Many public lands, which had little value and were unwanted in the past, are now extremely valuable. A failure to privatize these lands in the past, in spite of their low value at the time, is a major reason for government ownership problems today. If they had been given away, then taxpayers today would not be bearing the burdens of inefficient and wasteful government management. Such mistakes should be avoided in the future.

Conclusions

There is no philosophical or intellectual justification for government ownership and management of timberlands in the U. S., which has a free enterprise (market) economic system. Government timber production is a collectivist institutional arrangement that is incompatible with free enterprise.

The U. S. has institutionalized an anomalous situation in this regard because of historical misinterpretations of the costs of economic growth and development. A poor understanding of the economics of natural resources and timber inventory management led to incorrect diagnoses of the social costs of alienating public domain timberlands into private ownership—and further, to major policy mistakes.

More is known about these issues today. Given this additional knowledge and the benefits of hindsight, the conclusion seems inescapable that the American people blundered into a socialized system of timber management. For over half a century, its existence mattered little. Government timber management was largely custodial. Most timber was produced from privately owned stands located closer to markets and wood-processing facilities.

Private timber inventories were depleted, however, and since several decades are required to grow new timber crops, wood-processing industries and the housing industry have become heavily dependent upon government timber. As this dependency progressed, economic disruptions have increased, largely because of reduced timber supplies and the supply rigidity created by the even flow concept.

Most economists who have examined the even flow concept consider it a wasteful economic absurdity. It does not promote stability, as government foresters allege. In fact, it is destabilizing. It also precludes economical management of government timber inventories. Government timber production tends to be grossly overcapitalized, a consequence of both even flow and a failure to count interest carrying charges on timber (capital) assets.

Nor can the even flow concept be justified on the basis of multiple-use benefits. Such arguments for government ownership are more rationalization than justification. Private timberlands produce multiple-use benefits too, and they do so much more efficiently than do those of government.

If society wants a different mix of multiple-use outputs than would be produced if government timberlands were privatized, this should be made known and the appropriate steps taken to ensure optimal outputs. Easements can be used for this purpose. The important point is to create a system of incentives to ensure that whatever output is desired will be produced efficiently.

Private ownership is the best means of assuring productive efficiency.

82

Government ownership of commercial timber resources is demonstrably inefficient and wasteful, although the extent to which this is so is disguised by poor accountability.

Clemenceau once observed that "war is too important to leave to the generals." Government forest management, it would appear, is becoming too important to leave to the foresters—especially in view of the poor results that their theories are producing and their reluctance to change them.

Changing institutional arrangements is not easy, for, once established, vested interests quickly follow. In the management of government timberlands vested interests have had nearly a century to become entrenched. They are sufficiently powerful and influential today to frustrate a meaningful dialogue on the issue of government timber production, and whether or not it might have been a mistake in the first place. Many government foresters continue to assert claims for the even flow concept that are patently false, and they commonly take refuge in laws that they themselves recommended to Congress and the state legislatures.

Except under the stress of obvious and serious malfunction, society has remained largely unconcerned with these matters. The timber industry is in serious trouble today, however, and policy reforms are badly needed. In addition, taxpayers have become increasingly reluctant to carry the burdens of unnecessary and wasteful government activities.

The solution to the problems that have been created by government timber production will not be found in larger agency budgets or the adoption of more laws and regulations, both of which have numerous supporters. Privatization is the only reform alternative compatible with the U. S. economic system and the overall goals of the American people.

Government should be removed from the business of producing timber. The free enterprise system has demonstrated convincingly that it can handle this task much more efficiently. Privatization of commercial government timberlands would relieve society of an unnecessary and costly tax burden, the magnitude of which can only increase. Perhaps more important, all Americans would benefit from the expanded freedom provided by the restoration of private property rights and the free enterprise system.

9

On Privatizing the Public Domain
by Steve H. Hanke

"Good has only one way, while evil has a thousand."

Balzac
Traité de la vie élégante

As we all know, the institution of private property has been a constant source of debate, even of wars. One group of protagonists has been the communists. This group does not accept either the form or the substance of private property. The original liberals, or what are today authentic conservatives, represent the opposite group. Authentic conservatives believe that private property—both in its form and substance—provides the cornerstone for a free society. An alleged member of this group, President Reagan—in his address of June 8, 1982, before both Houses of the British Parliament—asked the following question: "Who would voluntarily...opt for land to be owned by the state instead of those who till it...."

In between these two groups are the pragmatists, or moderates from either the left or the right, who operate on two artificially separated planes, the theoretical and the practical, with conflicting results. First, there are the socialists of all varieties. Although they are against the institution of private property, they believe that it is not practical to do away with the institution directly. Hence, the socialists do not oppose the form of private property. Rather, they attack its substance through the imposition of government controls. The result is a limitation of the freedom to use private property in a responsible manner.

The second group of pragmatists is traditional conservatives. In principle, they are strong believers in private property. However, they argue that this goal is not realistic. In fact, like the socialists, these conservatives accommodate themselves with limitations on private property. While socialists propose and push for collectivization, these conservatives only attempt to slow down that process.

What is correct and practical is to steer a new course, rather than simply retard the tidal wave of socialist proposals. An example of a new course involves specific policies to privatize federal government grazing lands by transferring them from public to private ownership.

Until the passage of the Taylor Grazing Act in 1934, the public domain was operated as a large commons. Since the Act, a more orderly method of utilization has been in effect. For the right to use public grazing lands, which cover approximately 155 million acres, ranchers must acquire grazing permits. To obtain these permits, ranchers must pay annual rents to the U.S. Government. By custom, the grazing permits, which number approximately 20,000, are *attached* to specific *parcels* of *private* land.

The linkage between public permits and private land has had a profound impact on the market for private land. The annual public grazing fees have been set below market-clearing levels. As a result, the grazing permit market has been cleared—supply has been equated with demand—not through the public grazing permit market itself, but through the market for the private lands that are linked to public permits. So, the difference between the public grazing fees that are charged and those that would clear the market for grazing permits has been capitalized into the value of the private lands that permits are attached to.

The linkage, through the capitalization process, between the market for public permits and that for private land, has important implications. With the exception of those who obtained the original permits, all ranchers have had to pay two prices for their public permits—a public price, in the form of an annual grazing fee, and a private price, in the form of a premium for their private lands.

Perhaps this linkage and the capitalization process can be better understood with a more familiar example: rent controls in New York City. Rents are controlled at levels below market-clearing levels. To clear the market for scarce housing space, the owners often require tenants to purchase (at an uncontrolled price) the furniture in the apartment. In this case, the difference between the rent controlled rent and the market-clearing rent is capitalized into the value of the furniture that is attached to the apartment. Hence, to purchase the right to use a rent controlled apartment, the tenants must pay two prices: a lump-sum premium for the furniture and a monthly apartment rental that is set below the market-clearing level.

To privatize public grazing lands and transfer public grazing permits (surface rights) to private ranchers on an equitable basis, a lump-sum amount should be charged to ranchers. This charge should be set so that it is equivalent, in present value terms, to the amount that the U.S. government would receive in grazing fees over time if the government retained title to the lands and continued to charge an annual grazing fee or rent. In effect, the government would be put in a position in which it is indifferent between receiving a lump-sum payment today or a stream of annual rents over time. Moreover, ranchers would be charged for only that portion of the permits' value that had not already been paid for through premiums for private land.

This can be accomplished in the following manner. Each rancher could be given an option to purchase, on a first-refusal basis, the public grazing permits that he now rents from the government. The first-refusal price would be set by capitalizing (at a one percent real rate of interest) the annual grazing fees (an annual average paid over the past five years in 1982 dollars) that the rancher has paid. One percent is an estimate of the real long-term interest rate paid by the U.S. Treasury, and the five-year average is an estimate of future annual fee payments. If the rancher should refuse to exercise his option, then the permits would be sold to the highest bidder, and the rancher should be compensated for the lost value of his lease-hold rights. This compensation would be equal to the difference between the highest bid price and the calculated first-refusal price.

A concrete example shows how to compute the first-refusal price. The ranch in the illustration is operated as a single unit. However, its lands are distributed in the following ownership pattern: 4,816 acres are privately owned; 8,333 acres are owned by the state government; and 1,520 acres are Section 15 lands, which are owned by the federal government. Our purpose is to calculate the first-refusal price for the federal lands. Table 1 summarizes the steps required to make this calculation.

Table 1
First-Refusal Price for Grazing Land: A Real Example
Step 1: Adjust Lease Payments to 1982 Dollars

(1) Year	(2) Payments in Current $	(3) Inflation Adjustment Factor	(4) = (2) × (3) Payments in 1982 $
1977	$616	1.50	$ 924
1978	616	1.41	869
1979	771	1.31	1,010
1980	963	1.20	1,156
1981	942	1.09	1,027

Step 2: Calculate Average Annual Lease Payment in 1982 $
Total Payments in 1982 $=$4,986
Total Number of Years=5
Average Annual Lease Payment 1982 $=$4,986/5=$997

Step 3: Capitalize Average Annual Lease Payment to Determine First-Refusal Price
Average Annual Lease Payment in 1982 $=$997
Capitalization Factor at 1% for 50 years=39.2
First-Refusal Price=$997×39.2=$39,079

Step 4: Calculate the First-Refusal Price Per Acre
Total First-Refusal Price=$39,079
Total Acres Under Lease=1,500
First-Refusal Price Per Acre=$39,079÷1,500=$26

The question now is: what would be the benefits associated with this privatization proposal?

First, the productivity of western ranchers would increase, since their costs per unit of output would fall. Moreover, consumers would be served more effectively. After all, the only way that private landowners can ultimately enjoy their property is to employ it for the satisfaction of other people's wants. The only way the ranchers can take advantage of what they own is to serve consumers. This, of course, is the social function that is served by private property.

Second, federal revenues would be generated. Instead of receiving annual grazing fees, the federal government would receive an equivalent lump-sum payment.

Third, the annual federal costs (and these do not include, as they should, capital carrying charges) exceed the annual revenues generated from federal grazing lands. Therefore, privatization would eliminate negative cash flows for the federal government. This would obviously benefit all U.S. taxpayers, who must now pay taxes to support the federal government's retention of public grazing lands.

Lastly, a state and local tax base would be created. Western dependence on Washington, D.C., would be reduced and federalism would be enhanced.

Traditional conservatives should join authentic conservatives in being innovative, dynamic and in steering a new course toward privatization. Privatization in all its forms, whether it be for material objects or intellectual creations, not only is the correct course in principle, but is also practical and beneficial. Repeated experiences show that any form of socialism provides the road to a collectivist society with its corollary, tyranny. The only road to liberty begins with privatization.

Bibliography

Ackerman, B. A., and W. T. Hassler. *Clean Coal/Dirty Air, or How the Clean-Air Act Became a Multibillion-Dollar Bail-Out for High Sulfur Coal Producers and What Should Be Done About It* (New Haven: Yale University Press, 1981).

Alchian, Armen, and Harold Demsetz. "Property Rights Paradigm." *Journal of Economic History* 33 (March 1973).

Anderson, Fredrick R. et al. *Environmental Improvement Through Economic Incentives* (Baltimore: John Hopkins University Press, 1977).

Anderson, Terry L., ed. *Water Resources: Bureaucracy, Property Rights, and the Environment* (Cambridge: Ballinger and Pacific Institute for Public Policy Research, 1982).

Anderson, Terry L., and P. J. Hill. "The Evolution of Property Right: A Study of the American West." *Journal of Law and Economics* 18 (April 1975), 163-79.

_____. "Toward a General Theory of Institutional Change." *Frontiers of Economics* (Blacksburg, Va.: University Publications, 1976), 3-18.

_____. *The Birth of a Transfer Society* (Stanford, Calif.: Hoover Institution Press, 1980).

Anglides, S., and E. Bardach. *Water Banking: How to Stop Wasting Agricultural Water* (San Francisco: Institute for Contemporary Studies, 1978).

Baden, John A., and Richard L. Stroup. "The Environment Costs of Government Action." *Policy Review* (Spring 1978), 23-26.

_____, eds. *Bureaucracy vs. Environment: The Environmental Costs of Bureaucratic Governance* (Ann Arbor: University of Michigan Press, 1981).

_____. "Entrepreneurship, Energy, and the Political Economy of Hope." *Exploration and Economics of the Petroleum Industry*. Proceedings of the Southwestern Legal Foundation. Vol. 19 (New York: Matthew Bender, 1981).

_____. *Natural Resources: Bureaucratic Myths and Environmental Management* (Cambridge: Ballinger and Pacific Institute for Public Policy Research, 1982).

_____. "Saving the Wilderness: A Radical Proposal." *Reason* 13:3 (July 1981), 28-36.

_____, and Walter Thurman. "Myths, Admonitions and Rationality: The American Indian as a Resource Manager." *Economic Inquiry*[19] (January 1981), 132-43.

Baumol, William J., and Walace E. Oates. *Economics, Environmental Policy, and the Quality of Life* (Englewood Cliffs, N.J.: Prentice-Hall, 1979).

89

Borcherding, T. E., ed. *Budgets and Bureaucrats: The Sources of Government Growth* (Durham, N.C.: Duke University Press, 1977).

Boskin, Michael J., ed. *The Crisis in Social Security: Problems and Prospects* (San Francisco: Institute for Contemporary Studies, 1977).

Buchanan, James, and Gordon Tullock. *The Calculus of Consent* (Ann Arbor: University of Michigan Press, 1962).

Burt, Oscar R. "Groundwater Management Under Institutional Restrictions." *Water Resources Research* 6:6 (1970), 1540–48.

Campbell, Colin D., ed. *Financing Social Security* (Washington, D.C.: American Enterprise Institute, 1979).

Cheung, Steven. "The Structure of a Contract and the Theory of a Non-Exclusive Resource." *Journal of Law and Economics* 3 (1970), 49–70.

Clawson, Marion. *Forests: For Whom and For What?* (Baltimore: Johns Hopkins, 1975).

—————. "The National Forests." *Science* 191 (1976), 762–67.

Coase, Ronald. "The Problem of Social Cost." *The Journal of Law and Economics* 4 (October 1960), 1–44.

Cuzan, Alfred. "A Critique of Collectivist Water Resources Planning." *Western Political Quarterly* 32:2 (September 1979).

Davis, Kenneth P. *Forest Management* (New York: McGraw-Hill, 1966).

De Alessi, Louis. "The Economics of Property Rights: A Review of the Evidence," *Research in Law and Economics*, Vol. 2, 1980, 1–47.

Demsetz, Harold. "Some Aspects of Property Rights." *Journal of Law and Economics* 9 (October 1966), 61–70.

—————. "Toward a Theory of Property Rights." *American Economic Review* 57 (May 1967), 347–59.

Duignan, Peter, and Alvin Rabushka, eds. *The United States in the 1980s.* (Stanford, Calif.: Hoover Institution Press, 1980).

Feldstein, Martin, ed. *The American Economy in Transition* (Chicago: University of Chicago Press, 1980).

Furubotn, Eirik and Svetozar Pejovich. "Property Rights and Economic Theory: A Survey of Recent Literature." *Journal of Economic Literature* 10 (1972), 1137–62.

Gardner, D. B. "Transfer Restrictions and Misallocation in Grazing Public Range." *Journal of Farm Economics* 44 (1962), 109–20.

Habicht, E. R. Jr. "Electric Utilities and Solar Energy: Competition, Subsidies, Ownership, and Prices." In *The Solar Market: Proceedings of the Symposium on Competition in the Solar Energy Industry* (Washington, D.C.: Federal Trade Commission, 1978).

Hardin, Garrett, and John Baden. *Managing the Commons* (San Francisco: Freeman, 1977).

Hotelling, Harold. "The Economics of Exhaustible Resources." *Journal of Political Economy* 39:2 (April 1939).

Hyde, William F. *Timber Supply and Forestland Allocation* (Baltimore: Johns Hopkins University Press, 1979).

Johnson, M. Bruce, ed. *Forestlands: Government Policy, Economic Performance, and the Environment* (Cambridge: Ballinger and Pacific Institute for
Public Policy Research, 1982).

Johnson, Ronald N., Micha Gisser and Michael Werner. "The Definition of a
Surface Water Right and Transferability." *Journal of Law and Economics*
24:2 (October 1981), 273–88.

Johnson, Ronald N., and Gary D. Libecap. "Agency Costs and the Assignment
of Property Rights: The Case of Southwestern Indian Reservations." *South-
ern Economic Journal* 47:2 (October 1980), 332–47.

_____. "Contracting Problems and Regulation: The Case of the Fishery,"
American Economic Review (December 1980).

_____. "Efficient Markets and Great Lakes Timber: A Conservation Issue
Reexamined," *Explorations in Economic History* (October 1980).

Kirzner, Israel. *Competition and Entrepreneurship* (Chicago: University of
Chicago Press, 1973).

Krueger, Anne O. "The Political Economy of the Rent Seeking Society." *American Economic Review* 64 (June 1974), 291–303.

Libecap, Gary D. "Bureaucratic Opposition to the Assignment of Property
Rights: Overgrazing on the Western Range," *Journal of Economic History*
(March 1980).

_____. "Economic Variables and the Development of the Law: The Case of
Western Mineral Rights." *Journal of Economic History* 38 (June 1978).

_____. *Locking Up the Range: Federal Land Controls and Grazing* (Cam-
bridge, Mass.: Ballinger and Pacific Institute for Public Policy Research,
1981).

_____ and Ronald N. Johnson. "Legislating Commons: The Navajo Tribal Council and the Navajo Range." *Economic Inquiry* 18:1 (January 1980), 69–86.

Maloney, M. T., and R. E. McCormick, "A Positive Theory of Environmental
Quality Regulation," *Journal of Law and Economics* (April 1982).

Mitchell, William. *The Anatomy of Government Failure* (Los Angeles: International Institute for Economic Research, 1979).

Niskanen, William A. *Bureaucracy and Representative Government* (Chicago:
Aldine, 1971).

_____. "Bureaucracies and Politicians." *Journal of Law and Economics*
18:3 (1975), 617–43.

North, Douglas. "A Framework for Analyzing the State in Economic History."
Explorations in Economic History 16 (1979), 249–59.

Olsen, Mancur Jr. *The Logic of Collective Action* (New York: Schocken Books,
1965).

Pejovich, Svetozar. *Fundamentals of Economics: A Property Rights Approach*
(Dallas: The Fisher Institute, 1979).

Peltzman, Sam. "Toward a More General Theory of Regulation." *The Journal
of Law and Economics* 11 (1976), 211–40.

Public Land Law Review Commission. *One Third of the Nation's Land* (Washington, D.C.: Government Printing Office, 1970).

Ruff, Larry E. "The Common Economic Sense of Pollution." *The Public Interest* 19 (Spring 1970), 69-85.

Schultze, C. *The Public Use of Private Interest* (Washington, D.C.: The Brookings Institution, 1977).

Smith, Vernon L. "The Primitive Hunter Culture." *Journal of Political Economy* 83 (August 1975), 727-56.

_____. "Water Deeds: A Proposed Solution to the Water Valuation Problem." *Arizona Review* 26 (January 1977), 7-10.

Stevens, Joe B., and E. Bruce Godfrey. "Use Rates, Resource Flows, and Efficiency of Public Investment in Range Improvements." *American Journal of Agriculture Economics* 54:4 (November 1972), 611-21.

Stigler, George. "The Theory of Economic Regulaton." *Bell Journal of Economics and Management Science* 2 (1971), 3-21.

Stroup, Richard L., and John A. Baden. "Externality, Property Rights, and the Management of Our National Forests." *Journal of Law and Economics* 16 (Spring 1973).

_____. "Property Rights and Natural Resource Management." *Literature of Liberty* 2 (October-December 1979), 5-44.

Tullock, Gordon. *The Politics of Bureaucracy* (Washington, D.C.: Public Affairs Press, 1965).

_____. *Private Wants and Public Means* (New York: Basic Books, 1970).

_____. "The Cost of Transfers." *Kyklos* 24 (1971), 629-43.

Weidenbaum, M. L. and R. Harnish *Government Credit Subsidies for Energy Development* (Washington, D.C.: American Enterprise Institute, 1976).

Yandle, Bruce. "The Emerging Market for Air Pollution Rights." *Regulation* (July-August 1978), 21-29.

Biographies

PHIL TRULUCK is currently the Executive Vice-President and Chief Operating Officer of The Heritage Foundation. He is a graduate of the University of South Carolina, where he also pursued graduate studies. Before joining The Heritage Foundation as Director of Research in 1977, Mr. Truluck was a research assistant to Senator Strom Thurmond (South Carolina), Special Assistant to Representative Ben Blackburn (Georgia), and Deputy Director of the Republican Study Committee.

JOHN BADEN is the Director of the Center for Political Economy and Natural Resources at Montana State University. He has a B.A. degree from Wittenberg University, and he received a Ph.D. in Political Science from Indiana University in 1969.

Specializing in political economy and public policy, Dr. Baden has taught at several universities, including Indiana State and Utah State. He has authored numerous articles, focusing on land use and environmental policies. He is on the Executive Council of the Western Political Science Association, and is a member of the Editorial Board of *Western Political Quarterly*.

MARION CLAWSON is a Senior Fellow Emeritus and Consultant at Resources For The Future. He received a B.S. from the University of Nevada and a Ph.D. from Harvard University. Dr. Clawson was a Visiting Professor at Duke University from 1977 to 1981, and a Regent's Professor at University of California, Berkeley, in 1976.

Dr. Clawson has received numerous honors and distinctions, and he is a Fellow of the American Academy of Arts and Sciences and an Honorary Member of the National Academy of Public Administration. He has authored many articles and books, including *Forests For Whom and For What?* and *New Deal Planning—National Resources Planning Board*.

BARNEY DOWDLE is currently Professor of Forest Resources and Adjunct Professor of Economics at the University of Washington. Dr. Dowdle received his B.S. degree from the University of Washington in 1957 and his Ph.D. degree from Yale University in 1962. He is a member of the national honors society, Phi Beta Kappa, and he belongs to several economic associations.

Dr. Dowdle specializes in natural resource economics and forestry management. He has served as a consultant to a variety of public and private agencies, and he currently advises the States' Rights Coordinating Council, an organization which supports the goals of the "Sagebrush Rebellion."

STEVE HANKE is former Senior Economist for the President's Council of Economic Advisors. He is on leave from Johns Hopkins University where he is a Professor of Applied Economics. In 1981, Dr. Hanke was the Distinguished Visiting Scholar at the Lund Institute of Technology, University of Lund in Sweden. He also is an Adjunct Scholar with The Heritage Foundation.

Dr. Hanke received both his B.S. and his Ph.D. from the University of Colorado in Boulder. He has authored numerous articles on land and water use. He is a member of the Advisory Council of the Political Economy Research Center in Bozeman, Montana.

BRUCE JOHNSON is Research Director for the Pacific Institute for Public Policy and is a Professor of Economics at the University of California, Santa Barbara. He received his B.A. from Carleton College in 1955 and his Ph.D. from Northwestern University in 1962.

Dr. Johnson's areas of expertise include public utility, environmental, and energy-related economics. He has authored and edited numerous works, including *The Environmental Cost of Bureaucratic Government* and *Resolving the Housing Crisis: Government Policy, Decontrol, and the Public Interest*. Dr. Johnson is a member of the Advisory Board of the Local Government Center and is a Trustee of The Reason Foundation. He recently was installed as President of the Western Economic Association.

GARY LIBECAP is currently Associate Professor of Economics at Texas A&M University. He received his B.A. from the University of Montana and his Ph.D. from the University of Pennsylvania. He has taught at several universities, including Columbia and Rutgers.

Dr. Libecap has written many articles and reviews for publications such as *Business History Review* and *Economic Inquiry*. He is the author of *The Evolution of Private Mineral Rights* and *Locking Up The Range*.

LOUIS PAUWELS founded *Le Figaro Magazine* in 1976 as a forum for leading opponents of Marxism and socialism. The magazine has become the number one French weekly, with a readership of over three million. One of the most effective opposition editorialists in France, Mr. Pauwels is a leader of the neoconservative movement in Europe. He also has authored several books and articles.

94

BERNARD SIEGAN is Distinguished Professor of Law and Director of Law and Economic Studies at the University of San Diego School of Law. He received his J.D. degree from the University of Chicago Law School, and he has been a practicing attorney since 1949.

Mr. Siegan has authored several books, including *Land Use Without Zoning*, *Other People's Property*, and *Economic Liberties and the Constitution*. He also has authored numerous articles, and he has edited several works, including *Government, Regulation, and the Economy*.

SENATOR STEVEN SYMMS of Idaho was elected to the United States Senate in 1980, after serving four terms in the House of Representatives. Currently, he serves on several Senate committees, including the Finance Committee, the Budget Committee, and the Environmental and Public Works Committee. Senator Symms chairs the Estate and Gift Taxation Subcommittee of the Senate Finance Committee and the Transportation Subcommittee of the Environmental and Public Works Committee.

A native of Idaho, Senator Symms earned a B.S. degree from the University of Idaho, and he served for three years in the U.S. Marine Corps. He is the recipient of numerous awards, including the 1976 and 1977 Statesman Awards from the American Conservative Union and the 1976 Liberty Award from the Congress of Freedom.

A vigorous advocate of limited government and the free enterprise system, Senator Symms has focused much of his legislative activity toward tax reform and federal spending reductions.

Thomas Sowell, Herman Kahn,
Eugene McCarthy, Raymond Aron,
Daniel Moynihan, Kingsley Amis,
Elliot Abrams, Ernest van den Haag,
Nathan Glazer, Tom Bethell, Luigi Barzini,
Michael Novak, Paul Craig Roberts,
Colin Gray, George Gilder,
Robert Conquest, Guenter Lewy,
Paul Johnson, Midge Decter, and
Milton Friedman are writing in *Policy
Review.* . . . **Why aren't you reading it?**

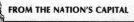